D1171855

Visual
COMMUNICATION
for the Hard of Hearing

371.912
ON2
HV
2487
.O5
1964

JOHN J. O'NEILL

Director, Speech and Hearing Clinics
University of Illinois

HERBERT J. OYER

Director, Speech and Hearing Clinics
Michigan State University

Visual COMMUNICATION

for the Hard of Hearing

· HISTORY · RESEARCH · METHODS

WITHDRAWN

Prentice–Hall, Inc.

ENGLEWOOD CLIFFS, N. J.

130090

© 1961 BY
PRENTICE-HALL, INC.
ENGLEWOOD CLIFFS, N. J.

94247-C

All rights reserved. No part of this book may be reproduced in any form, by mimeograph or any other means, without permission in writing from the publishers.

LIBRARY OF CONGRESS
CATALOG CARD NUMBER: 61-11206

PRINTED IN THE
UNITED STATES OF AMERICA

Third printing......June, 1964

TEACHING A COURSE DEVOTED TO LIPREADING POSES SEV-eral problems. The major one is the selection of a text for such specialized instruction. Usually eight to ten references are selected or an extensive bibliography is prepared. However, the bulk of these references merely present limited background information, extensive practice materials, and orientation to one specific method of teaching lipreading. There is no detailed account of the research recently accomplished, and there is no one source that provides a review of new lipreading methods or a suggested procedure to be used in the teaching of lipreading.

We have been involved in this struggle for several years. Out of our discontent and the anguish of our students grew a desire to co-ordinate the information scattered over the years and through the pages of numerous books and journals. We have chosen to use the term *lipreading* because of its historical usage and familiarity.

PREFACE

We do not wish the term to be considered an operational definition of the process; rather we want to use it in an organizational sense, to assist us in co-ordinating the information of the past and present.

The text is to serve two purposes. First, it will be a basic reference for a course devoted to aural rehabilitation, speech reading, or lipreading. Second, it will serve as a reference source for students of psychology, special education, and otology.

The authors wish to acknowledge the stimulation and interest evoked by Thomas B. Anderson who first introduced them to the complexities and fascinations of lipreading. Also, the spirit of the late Marie K. Mason was ever present during work with the hard of hearing. Finally, the many unanswered classroom questions provided by students must be acknowledged as "spurs to action."

JOHN J. O'NEILL
HERBERT J. OYER

1. 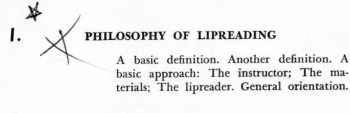 PHILOSOPHY OF LIPREADING   1

      A basic definition. Another definition. A basic approach: The instructor; The materials; The lipreader. General orientation.

2.   HISTORICAL ASPECTS   9

      Through past centuries. More recent developments in Europe. Early development in America. More recent development in America: Bruhn; Nitchie; Kinzie; Others. Present status of lipreading.

3.   TESTS OF LIPREADING   20

      Review of formal lipreading tests. Informal assessment of lipreading ability. Factors to consider in constructing a test of lipreading: The population to be tested; General format of the test; Selection of speakers; Selection of test items; Test conditions; Scoring procedure. Summary.

TABLE OF CONTENTS

4. THE EXPERIMENTAL STUDY OF
LIPREADING   35

> The lipreader or receiver: Intelligence; Be-
> havioral patterns; Visual skills; Miscella-
> neous. The environment. Code or stimulus
> materials. The speaker or sender. Glossary.

5. VISUAL TRAINING AND VISUAL
METHODS   50

> A suggested approach: Visual perception; At-
> tention span; Concentration. Motion pic-
> tures.

6. LIPREADING, AUDITORY TRAINING
AND HEARING AIDS   70

> Areas to be considered in combined practice:
> Equipment; Materials. Suggested approach
> utilizing lipreading and hearing. The use of
> hearing aids. Outline of first four weeks of
> an aural rehabilitation program.

7. LIPREADING METHODS AND
MATERIALS FOR CHILDREN   84

> Methods: Bruhn; Kinzie; Brauckmann. Ma-
> terials: Stowell, Samuelson, and Lehman;
> Whildin and Scally; Samuelson and Fabre-
> gas; New aids and materials for teaching lip-
> reading; Beginning lip reading; Yenrick;
> Hearing with our eyes; Stories and games
> for easy lipreading practice; Morkovin and
> Moore; Whitehurst.

8. LIPREADING METHODS AND
MATERIALS FOR ADULTS   93

> Methods: Nitchie; Bruhn; Kinzie; Brauck-
> mann. Summary of methods. Materials: Mor-
> genstern; Mason; Montague; The Deshon
> book; Morkovin and Moore; Ordman and
> Ralli; Faircloth; Feilbach; Fisher; Ewing.

9. **AN APPROACH TO PLANNING OF LIPREADING LESSONS** 106

Cases and discussion. General suggestions for lipreading lesson planning.

10. **ASSIGNMENTS AND ADVICE TO PARENTS** 117

Adult assignments. Children's assignments. Advice to parents: Parental group conference

11. **TELEVISION AND LIPREADING INSTRUCTION** 130

Possible values of television. Possible use of television: Educational or Commercial television; Closed-circuit television; Characteristics of the instructor; A pilot program.

APPENDIXES 141

A. Visual hearing tests for children. B. Visual hearing films. C. Practice activities.

Visual COMMUNICATION

for the Hard of Hearing

1

LIPREADING, SPEECH READING, OR VISUAL HEARING ARE ALL terms that have been used to describe a particular form of nonauditory communication. In normal oral communication the articulators—the tongue, lips, and teeth —serve as modulators of the air stream. The resulting modulations take form as consonants and vowels which the ear of a listener receives and passes on for interpretation in the higher brain centers. However, for the individual with a moderate to severe hearing loss, the visual shape and movement of a speaker's articulators become the important communicative elements. In this situation the eye is the primary receptor, with the ear affording some slight assistance. Thus, an additional sensory pathway can be used by a person who is aurally handicapped.

PHILOSOPHY OF LIPREADING

A Basic Definition

In terms of present teaching methods, the correct recognition of the movement of the articulators is not the only goal of lipreading instruction. The complete and desired goal is to carry on communication with the same degree of meaningfulness as would be obtained with auditory transmission. Through the years there has been no clear-cut definition of lipreading which takes into account such an end product. Therefore the following operational definition is offered: *lipreading is the correct identification of thoughts transmitted via the visual components of oral discourse.* This can be shortened to *visual thought comprehension.* The basic change in orientation required by such an assumption is that lip movements transmit thoughts or meaning. It is recognized that the use of the concept *meaning* can lead to problems of definition. However, Osgood *et al.*[1] have provided a clear interpretation of the process or processes involved in the development of meaning. Their explanation states that

> a pattern of stimulation which is not the significate is a sign of that significate if it evokes in the organism a mediating process; this process (a) being some fractional part of the total behavior elicited by the significate, and (b) producing responses which would not occur without the previous contiguity of non-significate and significate patterns of stimulation.

Such an explanation also serves in many respects, as a description of the lipreading process. It is interesting to note here that little effort has been made to use such psychological constructs or the results of psychological research to describe or explain lipreading.

In terms of historical development it is possible to depict the various approaches that have been used in the teaching of lipreading. Figure 1 illustrates a method that might be called *analytical.*

Another approach is depicted in Figure 2. This figure portrays the so-called *synthetic* approach.

However, the following type of teaching approach is more synthetic.

$$\left.\begin{array}{l}\text{Key Vocabulary} \\ \text{Identified Context} \\ \text{Knowledge of Linguistic Rules}\end{array}\right\} = \text{Thought}$$

---

[1] C. E. Osgood, G. J. Suci, and P. H. Tannenbaum, *The Measurement of Meaning* (Urbana: University of Illinois Press, 1957), p. 7.

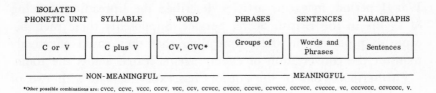

FIGURE 1. *Representation of the analytical approach to the teaching of lipreading.*

In this instance emphasis is placed upon recognition of thoughts or the reception of meaningful materials. If we borrow from some of the phrases used by Allport[2] in his review of perceptual theories, we might say that lip movements have concrete object character. In much simpler words, lip movements represent meaning. If we accept such an orientation, lipreading must be considered as a form

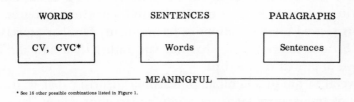

FIGURE 2. *Representation of the synthetic approach to the teaching of lipreading.*

of learned behavior; or more specifically, it must be considered as a form of perceptual behavior that requires the visual modality to handle, not printed words but another form of symbolism—the lip movements that are observed as language units. A lipreader would be unable to interpret visual movements without a knowledge of the meaning of such movements. Just as the young child with normal hearing must learn to associate auditory signals with various referents, the lipreader must learn to associate visual symbols with their referents. Thus, lipreading is a form of learned, linguistic behavior.

The primary argument raised against the view that lipreading is a form of learned behavior is that it apparently cannot be taught.

[2] F. H. Allport, *Theories of Perception and the Concept of Structure* (New York: John Wiley and Sons, Inc., 1955), p. 64.

Learning in this instance has been *considered* as a change in performance associated with practice. However, during the World-War-II period, magazine articles described the lipreading training of agents in the British Secret Service. Supposedly these men became so proficient in their lipreading that they could effectively monitor the conversation of enemy agents seated across the room.

Furthermore, one of the authors has experimented with two of his children, ages eight and nine, to discover if they could learn to lipread a strange, limited vocabulary. The vocabulary consisted on one occasion of strange personal names, and another time, of the names of odd foods we would not like to eat. In one of the more erudite moments, French phrases with appropriate gestures were used. Apparently, these two youngsters developed sufficient skill to utilize this lipreading as a dinner-table game. Also, both of the authors in their clinical contacts have been able to build a communicative situation to the extent that a visible vocabulary has been learned. These communication situations consisted of verbal exchanges that could occur at the drug store, or in a discussion of a favorite automobile, favorite foods, and favorite cigarettes. The clients viewed these situations as having many familiar aspects, and they became interested in what was said rather than how the information appeared on the lips.

Several techniques familiar to learning theorists, that is, development of preparatory set, association, and reinforcement, have been employed in such training. As an example of each of these areas, it would be well to describe the development of a lipreading lesson. The client is shown a picture depicting a specific situation. For example, a *Saturday Evening Post* cover depicting a family loading up their automobile for a summer vacation trip served as the focal point of a lesson. The therapist, using voice, pointed out the topics that the picture could bring to mind. Then, with a preface such as "Now let us see what these people might be saying," the practice material was presented without voice. The client had been prepared; he had a *preparatory set* for what was to follow. During the presentation of the lesson, each section was organized in such a fashion that each was a continuation of the basic thought presented in the previous section. Thus *association* in terms of referral to previous items, or thoughts, could be utilized. The therapist, by the use of voice or gestures, or by reference to self or others, assisted the client to develop an orientation to the topic under discussion. Thus the client was able to associate the therapist's structuring activity with the practice materials to follow. *Reinforcement,* or reward for correct recognition, occurred when the therapist indicated to the client that he had understood the basic thought being transmitted. Also, the therapist pre-structured[3] the practice materials through the use of voice, gestures, and paraphrases in such a manner that the client could follow the progress of thoughts up to the correct response. Thus the client, through the very action of following the progression of thoughts, was given reinforcement in terms of obvious, successful experience.

In this way, a form of behavior using visible symbols is manipulated. The manner in which such a stimulus is perceived must be affected by past experience. If we do not accept the assumption that lipreading is a form of learned behavior, we must assume that it is a trait. It would then be necessary to bring in the geneticist to decide which Mendelian law accounts for the transmission of such a trait!

Another Definition

It is evident that there is a need for a new term to describe what is done by an orally handicapped observer when he is communicating with another person. Terms such as *lipreading* or *speech reading* are not satisfactory because they restrict function. Mason[4] attempted to resolve this problem by employing the term *visual hearing.* In the case of an aurally handicapped individual, the eye, not the ear, functions in the comprehension of spoken thought; thus Mason felt that *visual hearing* was far more descriptive of such a form of communication. The process was considered to be twofold: phonetic and mental.

It is possible to modify Mason's viewpoint and describe a process known as *visual listening.* The relatively new discipline of listening has assumed an important role in the areas of communication training and research. Nichols and Stevens[5] have pointed out that passive

[3] Pre-structuring involves prior analysis on the part of the therapist who breaks down the communication situation into its simplest components. The student is informed of the nature of the situation, the topic, and the people and objects that will be involved in the practice materials. The client is led into lipreading in that he has been gaining information via lipreading. Thus, when he arrives at the actual practice material, he has an expectancy that he will be able to lipread and that what he is lipreading is a continuation of an information-sharing process.

[4] M. K. Mason, "A Cinematographic Technique for Testing Visual Speech Comprehension," *Journal of Speech Disorders,* 8 (1943), pp. 271-278.

[5] R. G. Nichols and L. A. Stevens, *Are You Listening?* (New York: McGraw-Hill Book Company, Inc., 1959).

hearing is not the ideal or most efficient method to be used in the obtaining and retaining of orally presented information. The authors stress that listening requires a learned approach. The results of their research indicate that specific factors are related to skill in listening. These factors include the size of the listener's vocabulary, his ability to grasp main ideas as opposed to specific facts, his ability to make inferences, and lastly, a definite interest in the material being discussed. Recent experimentation in the neurophysiology of hearing[6] has been directed toward an analysis of the functions of the brain during attention to sound. The results of the studies indicate that an attentive animal displays more activity in more brain locations than does the inattentive animal. Thus, there is a definite attention phenomenon common to auditory experience.

Wendell Johnson,[7] speaking for the area of general semantics, has described the act of listening as follows:

> . . . in order to cultivate the art of listening, one must at least relax and hear the speaker out—with a permissive understanding attitude, disregarding the speaker's symbols of authority, or lack of them, all the while asking, "what does he mean?," "How does he know?," and "what is he leaving out?"

Again, the basic point is that listening is a learned form of behavior, and this premise is vitally important in the development of attitudes and the accumulation of knowledge.

In lipreading there is a similarity between auditory and visual performance. A subject views a stimulus and attributes organization or meaning to what he sees. In other words, he views lip movements with the intent to understand the thoughts of a speaker, and attention is directed toward comprehension rather than mere recognition. Thus one may apply the descriptive but paradoxical term *visual listening*. The authors do not propose to adopt the term, but present it as a point of orientation.

A Basic Approach

In an analysis of the teaching of lipreading, there are three obvious areas to consider: the teacher or speaker, the stimulus, and the

[6] R. Galambos, "Some Recent Experiments on the Neurophysiology of Hearing," *Annals of Otology, Rhinology and Laryngology*, 65 (1956), pp. 1053-1059.

[7] W. Johnson, "Two Views on Listening: I. Do You Know How to Listen?", *ETC: A Review of General Semantics*, 7, (1) (1949), pp. 3-9.

student or receiver. The goal of the instructor is to present the material to the student in such a way that it can be correctly recognized. (The instructor can mouth words, present words with auditory amplification, use visual aids, or simplify the materials.) In addition, the stimulus materials and the set or preparation of the student should be considered. The receiver, or student, must develop an expectancy for the content of the stimulus materials and rely on his past experiences to perceive the stimulus. The materials should be familiar and fit into the expectancy and experience patterns of the viewer. Emphasis must be placed on comprehension rather than recognition. Thus, by using sensory pre-conditioning and directed practice, the instructor will expand the viewer's knowledge of language situations and reinforce the desired response pattern.

In summary form, the following requirements hold for the three areas of instruction under discussion:

The instructor should have an expressive face, flexible articulators, and some ability to use gestures. Also, before each presentation of stimulus materials, he must anticipate the student's difficulties, and prepare paraphases so that the viewer is kept lipreading. A knowledge of people, current events and local news is beneficial, as well as a great deal of patience and a firm belief in the philosophy that the aurally handicapped can be taught to lipread.

The materials should be meaningful, or complete thought units, and relate to the experiences of the viewer. They should be simple enough to be paraphrased or they should be keyed to a central thought.

The lipreader develops a preparatory set which alerts his visual scanning system to receive all lip movements as significant communicative materials. Thus he must not only utilize the lip movements but the situational cues, the context of the ongoing communication, and his knowledge of the interests and backgrounds of the speaker. Also, he must be prepared to assemble segmented information, always keeping in mind that a speaker delivers *information*, be it question, exposition or pun.

General Orientation

Lipreading instruction should be approached with a definite orientation and with definite goals. First, in the operational units or skills involved in the act of lipreading, the essential unit is that of visual skill. Therefore, training in visual perception is a vital part of lip-reading instruction. The next unit to consider is the set of the viewer. He must be trained to recognize that the visual events (lip movements) are meaningful language elements, and not mere isolated configurations. The training program should also include careful structuring of lesson materials, full utilization of residual hearing, and contextual organization of each lesson.

In addition, knowledge of the personality and aptitudes of the individual or group being trained is important. Not only must the instructor adapt the level of the stimulus materials to the abilities of those in training, but also he should present them in an informal manner, geared to the speech and interests of the individual or group. Also, it is necessary for the instructor to consider the viewer's past communication experience, his general sociability, and his ability to interact in social situations.

Only a trained instructor can manage such an approach; but the mere knowledge of lipreading techniques and their rote application will not suffice. The instructor must be professionally trained in the psychology of the aurally handicapped, the dynamics of human behavior, the functioning of the hearing mechanism, and the theoretical and practical aspects of aural rehabilitation. Here the term clinician, rather than instructor or teacher, becomes more meaningful, as it suggests a professionally trained person equipped to deal with the problems of the aurally handicapped and able to apply specific learning approaches at crucial moments.

A philosophy of lipreading has been presented. The philosophy stresses that lipreading is a form of learned behavior, not the mere reading of lip movements. Since the area of instruction is a professional one with a body of theoretical and experimental information, it is necessary for professionally trained individuals to apply the principles of training outlined in this text.

2

THE PURPOSE OF THIS CHAPTER IS TO PRESENT THE STU-
dent with a review of the development of lipreading in
Europe and America. One of the most complete works
on its history from early times until the latter 1920's is
The Story of Lip-Reading, by Fred Deland[1] who was
superintendent of the Volta Bureau from 1914-1922.
DeLand's work was revised and completed by Harriet
Montague.

The growth of lipreading is inextricably interwoven
with that of the education of the deaf. For many years
the deaf were considered lacking in intellect and incapa-
ble of learning, but once training programs were established for them, lipreading gradually began to be
taught. Today both the deaf and hard of hearing may
have the advantage of lipreading instruction, provided
those responsible for their programs do not rule it out
as being inferior to finger spelling and signs.

[1] Fred DeLand, *The Story of Lip-Reading* (Washington, D.C.: The
Volta Bureau, 1931).

HISTORICAL ASPECTS

Through Past Centuries

Presumably, an observation of Aristotle's prevented the deaf from being treated as intelligent human beings. He said that even though the deaf had voice, they were speechless. This simple statement was mistranslated and misinterpreted to the extent that it came to mean those born deaf were mentally deficient. The Latin Lucretius,[2] too, penned:

> To instruct the deaf no art could ever reach,
> No care improve them, and no wisdom teach.

However, early in the sixteenth century, the speculative Italian philosopher and physician, Jerome Cardan,[3] shattered the belief concerning the futility of educating the deaf, by demonstrating that their organs of speech could be made effective. A Spanish contemporary, Pedro Ponce de Leon, also believed that the deaf were educable, and he is considered their first teacher. From that time on, there was a progressive increase in educational opportunities for the acoustically handicapped. In some of the new schools, lipreading was undertaken; in others, manual language was stressed. Regardless of the fact that both the manual and oral methods were being taught, the important factor was that the aurally handicapped were finally being trained.

The first known book dealing with the oral method was *The Method of Teaching Deaf Mutes to Speak*,[4] written by Juan Pablo Bonet and published in Madrid in 1620. Bonet was interested in lipreading, but he did not feel that it could be taught to everyone; he felt that it was an art which could be acquired by only a few deaf persons. He reasoned that if enough time was spent practicing the art, the successful pupil would learn to lipread his *teacher,* but that he would probably be unable to transfer his training to other lipreading situations.

Twenty-eight years after the publication of the Bonet book, John Bulwer, an English physician, wrote *Philocopus, or The Deafe and Dumbe Man's Friend*.[5] Bulwer felt that lipreading could be taught to the deaf, but more important, that it was an avenue through which the deaf could learn to speak. His Scotch contemporary,

[2] E. A. Fay, "What Did Lucretius Say?" *American Annals of the Deaf,* 57 (1912), 213.
[3] *The Story of Lip-Reading, op. cit.,* p. 19.
[4] Fred DeLand, "Ponce de Leon and Bonet," *Volta Review,* 22 (1920), pp. 391-421.
[5] *The Story of Lip-Reading, op. cit.,* p. 41.

George Dalgarno, was not so enthusiastic toward lipreading. Dalgarno said in his Book, *Didascalocophus, or the Deaf and Dumb Man's Tutor*,[6] that when the deaf understand the motion of the lips, they understand not as a result of the lip movements themselves, but as a result of a concurrence of circumstances—time, place, persons and so on. Instead of lipreading and speech, Dalgarno advocated using letters of the alphabet on the finger tips and palm of the hand. It is interesting to note that A. G. Bell used a similar system in the lettered glove which he employed with his first pupil, George Sanders.[7]

More Recent Development in Europe

Throughout the seventeenth and eighteenth centuries, interest in lipreading spread to various parts of Europe. Many books and treatises were published extolling its virtues, and crude but basic methods were established. Amman, Baker, Pereire, and l'Epee were among those who taught and wrote.[8]

Amman, a brilliant Swiss physician, was graduated with honors at the University of Basle in 1687 and, five years later, published a book entitled *Surdus Loquens*,[9] in which he described the course he followed in teaching deaf-mutes to speak and to lipread. Amman believed that deaf-mutes are mute because they are deaf, and he made great use of mirror practice in his teaching of both lipreading and speech. Most of his work was carried out in Haarlem and Amsterdam, Holland as he left his native Switzerland soon after he received his doctor's degree.

In 1720 an Englishman named Henry Baker,[10] naturalist, poet, and Fellow of the Royal Society, became interested in the instruction of a young deaf girl. He taught her to read, to write, and to lipread, and was so encouraged by his success that he started a small private school. Unlike some of his comtemporaries, who wrote in detail of the methods they employed, Baker did not divulge his techniques.

---

[6] George Dalgarno, *Didascalocophus, or the Deaf and Dumb Man's Tutor* (Theater in Oxford), 1680. Reprinted in *American Annals of the Deaf*, 9 (1857), pp. 15-64.

[7] *The Story of Lip-Reading, op. cit.*, pp. 57-58.

[8] *Ibid.*, pp. 60-64.

[9] John C. Amman, *A Dissertation On Speech* (London: Sampson Low, Marston, Low and Searle, 1873), p. 154. The notice and description of this English translation of *Surdus Loquens* by Dr. Charles Baker, Doncaster, England, appears in the *American Annals of the Deaf*, 19 (1874), pp. 31-34.

[10] *The Story of Lip-Reading, op. cit.*, p, 68.

In fact, they were so secret, that it was said he asked a bond of 100 pounds from each pupil to ensure their secrecy.

During the time of Baker, a Spaniard named Jacob R. Pereire was working with the deaf in France. He taught both the manual alphabet and lipreading. The French Academy of Science investigated Pereire's method of teaching, and subsequently, after a favorable report was published, he became recognized as an outstanding authority. However, Pereire also neglected to write down his approach, so today we know nothing of it. In 1929, 149 years after his death a memorial[11] was erected in Peniche, Portugal in his honor.

Another contributor to the education of the deaf was Charles M. de l'Epee,[12] born in 1712 and a contemporary of Pereire. Professionally trained as both a priest and a lawyer, l'Epee's greatest desire was to help the poor. He realized this wish in the early years of the eighteenth century when he began a school for the aurally handicapped children of Paris. He lived frugally and was loved by his pupils. He even conducted the school at his own expense. L'Epee realized the importance of teaching lipreading and speech to these children in order to restore them to society, but their great number forced him to teach the manual method.[13] His school was later subsidized by the French government and gained attention of the Emperor of Austria, who, through the help of l'Epee, established the first public institution for the deaf in Vienna in 1799. After l'Epee's death, Sicard took over the school and continued with the manual method.

As the manual method became firmly entrenched in France, the oral method was promoted in Germany by Samuel Heinicke (1729-1790).[14] He continually pointed out the virtues of the oral method over the manual approach, and believed that clear thought was possible for the deaf, only if they learned to speak. He also believed that the deaf could learn to understand speech by carefully watching the motion of a speaker's lips. Heinicke occupies the same place of importance in Germany as an educator of the deaf as Ponce de Leon

[11] Josephine B. Timberlake, "A Memorial to Jacob Rodriquez Pereire," *Volta Review,* 31 (1929).

[12] Luzerne Rae, "The Abbe De l'Epee," *American Annals of the Deaf,* 1 (1848), pp. 69-76.

[13] An English translation of *The True Method of Educating The Deaf and Dumb, Confirmed by Long Experience,* by Abbe De l'Epee, appears in the *American Annals of the Deaf,* 1 and 2 (1860).

[14] Luzerne Rae, "A Monument to Heinicke," *American Annals of the Deaf,* 1 (1848), pp. 166-170.

holds in Spain, l'Epee in France, Braidwood in Scotland, and Gallaudet in America. After Heinicke died, his sons-in-law assumed his work and switched from the oral to the manual method. The oral method was not taught in Germany again until the next century, when F. M. Hill (1805-1874), a forceful and influential educator of the deaf, revived it.

Thomas Braidwood[15] (1715-1806), a mathematics teacher, was one of the most important figures in Great Britain in the development of lipreading instruction. He became interested in a deaf youngster at the school and tried to teach the child to speak. Eventually, his work was confined to the education of the deaf. It was said that his pupils seemed to hear with their eyes. Actually, he was teaching them to read lips. One of his pupils was an American boy named Charles Green. His father, Francis Green, realized the importance of his son's schooling with Braidwood, and crusaded in England and America for public supported instruction of the deaf. When Thomas Braidwood died, his son, widow, and later his son's widow, carried on his work. At one time the family operated three schools—one in London, one in Edinburgh, and one in Birmingham.

Early Development in America

John Braidwood,[16] grandson of Thomas Braidwood, migrated to America to establish a school for the deaf. A wealthy Virginian, who had a number of deaf persons in his family, helped him set up a small school in Cobbs, Virginia, in 1815. Braidwood made a few successful attempts at conducting the little school, but eventually it had to be turned over to a more responsible person.

At the time Braidwood was establishing his school in Virginia, Thomas Gallaudet,[17] a Yale graduate and an ordained minister, became intensely interested in the education of the deaf. He went to England in 1817 to learn the Braidwood methods of instruction. The Braidwoods, however, did not wish Gallaudet to learn their method, then return to America and open a school that would compete with young Braidwood's in Virginia; so they offered him a position on the staff. Just at this time, Gallaudet heard Abbe Sicard

---

[15] Luzerne Rae, "Thomas Braidwood," *American Annals of the Deaf,* 3, 1851. pp 255-256.

[16] *The Story of Lip-Reading, op. cit.,* pp. 93-97.

[17] H. P. Peet, "Tribute to the Memory of the Late Thomas Gallaudet," *American Annals of the Deaf,* 4 (1852), pp. 65-77.

lecture in London, and told him of his wish to educate the deaf. Sicard persuaded Gallaudet to go to his school in Paris and learn the sign and finger-spelling method. With Gallaudet's decision to go to the Paris school, the future of many American deaf was determined, for Sicard advocated the manual method while the Braidwoods taught the oral. One can only speculate on the history of lipreading in America had Gallaudet remained in London and worked with the Braidwoods on speech and lipreading.

At the Sicard school Gallaudet became a friend of Laurent Clerc,[18] a deaf teacher. He told Clerc of the great need for teachers of the deaf in America, and after approximately two months of training, he and Clerc left France for America to open a school at Hartford, Connecticut. Clerc knew no English when he left France, but Gallaudet taught it to him on the 52-day voyage home. Four years later, the school they started had made such excellent progress, that it received federal subsidization and was established as the American Asylum for The Deaf, now the American School for The Deaf.

Other schools for the deaf were established in the United States, but these schools all adopted the manual approach because of its spectacular success, and because of the prevalent theory that the deaf were honestly unable to speak. DeLand [19] reports that gradually educators began to notice the success of the oral method as it was taught in England and Germany. In 1843, Horace Mann returned from Europe with favorable and enthusiastic reports on the oral approach, but advocators of the manual method did not weaken, and speech and lipreading were taught in only the smallest private schools. However, in 1867, the great philanthropist, John Clarke, donated $50,000 to help establish an oral school for the deaf in Northampton, Massachusetts. Two years after the opening of the Clarke School for the Deaf, an oral day school was founded in Boston. It was in this school that Alexander Graham Bell taught the Visible Speech Symbols that his father, Melville Bell, had originated. From this time on in America, lipreading education was given more consideration. The advocates of speech and lipreading soon became as spectacular in their art as were those highly skilled in the manual method. Lipreading, as a method of teaching the deaf to communicate, had at last found its proper place in America.

[18] W. W. Turner, "Laurent Clerc," *American Annals of the Deaf,* 15 (1870), pp. 16-28.
[19] *The Story of Lip-Reading, op. cit.,* p. 110.

The *American Annals of the Deaf and Dumb,* a magazine dealing with the earliest teaching of lipreading, was the official publication of the Convention of the American Instructors of the Deaf and Dumb, and was first printed in 1847 at the Hartford school. Today it is entitled *American Annals of the Deaf.* In 1899, the *Association Review,* later known as the *Volta Review,* was published by the American Association to Promote the Teaching of Speech to the Deaf. This periodical took its name from the Volta Prize established in France by Napoleon Bonaparte, in honor of the Italian scientist, Volta, who in 1800 invented a battery which would generate electricity chemically. In 1880, A. G. Bell won the Volta Prize money for his telephone invention, and used the money to set up a fund for the promotion of scientific research. In 1887, as a result of great success with his phonograph records, he was able to give his father, Melville Bell, $100,000 to create and maintain a bureau for increasing and diffusing knowledge concerning the deaf. Seven years later, the Volta Bureau was constructed in Washington, D.C. It gives information about the problems encountered by those who are partially or completely acoustically handicapped; it maintains a free placement service for teachers, publishes materials for use with the hard of hearing and deaf, and gives personal advice to the aurally handicapped seeking it throughout the world.

Until the 1890's the teaching of lipreading was largely confined to children; but soon adults were given the opportunity to learn with the children in small schools. One of the first teachers of adults was Lillie E. Warren. She trained her pupils to associate certain numbers with certain sounds. According to Warren, the sounds of English were revealed in sixteen facial configurations. The numbering of these configurations was the means by which she classified them. Warren referred to her approach as the *numerical cipher method.* Edward B. Nitchie, who later made significant contributions to the teaching of lipreading, was one of Miss Warren's assistants.

At a meeting of the American Association to Promote the Teaching of Speech to the Deaf in 1894, lipreading teaching received a new impetus. At this conference Mrs. A. G. Bell[20] presented a paper in which she called for more use of the synthetic approach in educating the deaf. Up to this time, emphasis had been placed upon teaching the student to analyze mouth positions as the various sounds were produced. She felt, instead, that the speech reader's

[20] *The Story of Lip-Reading, op. cit.,* p. 147.

primary aim should be to grasp a speaker's whole meaning, rather than to understand each word or even each sentence. Mrs. Bell was deaf, but had learned to speak and lipread early in childhood; she spoke from actual experience as a lipreader, and not as one interested in expanding a particular method.

More Recent Development in America

Most of the outstanding contributors to the teaching of lipreading in America since 1900 are advocates of specific methods, and some have written at length about their approaches.

Bruhn

One of the early twentieth century pioneers in lipreading was Martha Bruhn. While a teacher of foreign language in the public schools of Boston, she gradually lost her hearing and was forced to seek specialized medical and educational help. She made contact with Herr Julius Mueller-Walle in Germany and studied lipreading with him. She was so successful that in 1902 she founded her own school in America. The Bruhn method was based largely upon syllable drill and also upon close observation of the movements of the lips from one sound position to another.[21]

Nitchie

Another worker instrumental in bringing help to the deaf was Edward B. Nitchie, who became deaf himself when fourteen years of age. He studied under Warren, but after two years left her and in 1903 began teaching deaf children regular school subjects in a school he had opened in New York. The demand for lipreading instruction from acoustically handicapped adults increased so greatly that Nitchie directed his attention to the education of adults exclusively. He trained many teachers and was responsible for creating what is now the New York League for the Hard of Hearing. He published several books and also a small periodical entitled *Courage*. The little magazine carried articles on lipreading and success stories of deaf people. Nitchie worked hard to improve his method of teaching lipreading, and during a short span of years shifted from a

---

[21] Martha E. Bruhn, *The Mueller-Walle Method of Lip-Reading for the Deaf* (Lynn, Mass: The Nichols Press, 1929), pp. 2-6.

strictly analytical approach to a synthetic one.[22] He died at the age of forty, but his wife has carried on his work.

Kinzie

Still another leader in America during the early part of the twentieth century was Cora Kinzie.[23] A second year medical student when her hearing acuity diminished, she sought professional help in lipreading from Martha Bruhn. Her intent in learning to lipread was to continue her study of medicine. As her hearing lessened, she gave up her medical studies and turned to the teaching of lipreading as a career. She first took the Bruhn normal course, then in 1914 she opened the Mueller-Walle School of Lipreading in Philadelphia. While in Philadelphia, she decided to increase her own lipreading effectiveness by studying with Nitchie in New York City. As a result, she evolved her own method, a combination of those taught by Nitchie and Bruhn. From Bruhn she incorporated classification of introductory sounds, and from Nitchie some basic psychological ideas. Shortly thereafter, Cora's sister, Rose, a public school teacher, joined the school, and they renamed it the "Kinzie School of Speech Reading." They soon increased their enrollment and became well known for their successful efforts with the acoustically handicapped. Their Speech Reading Club at one time had a membership of approximately 850 people.[24] After six years of activity, the sisters sold their school and retired to develop a series of graded lessons in lipreading. Their book in 1929 was the first of this series. The lessons were constructed to provide materials for lipreaders of varying abilities. The series runs from I through VIII, with I, II, and III for children and IV for adult beginners. Series V, VI, VII, and VIII were structured for advanced adults.

Others

Between 1900 and 1930, several others made notable contributions to lipreading in America. Jacob Reighard, Bessie Whitaker, and Anna Bunger were instrumental in introducing the method of Karl Brauckmann of Jena, Germany. Reighard, of the University of Michigan, translated the Brauckmann work into English and in 1926

[22] Edward B. Nitchie, *Lip-Reading, Principles and Practice* (New York: Frederick A. Stokes Company, 1912), p. 20.
[23] Cora E. Kinzie and Rose Kinzie, *Lip-Reading For the Deafened Adult* (Chicago: The John C. Winston Co., 1931), pp. 57-65.
[24] *The Story of Lip-Reading, op. cit.*, p. 179.

persuaded Whitaker, a former student of Nitchie and Bruhn, to try out the method with newly formed adult lipreading classes at Michigan State Normal College in Ypsilanti. Bunger later prepared a text explaining the Jena method[25] which utilizes the kinaesthetic, as well as visual cues. The latter approach is based on a more scientific rationale than some of the others.

Since 1930, however, no distinctive methods have evolved. The procedures have been based on one or a combination of the early methods. The use of films has become more prevalent in teaching and research, but this use of films, in tests of lipreading, dates back to 1915.

Marie K. Mason worked diligently from the early 1930's until 1947 to develop a film technique for teaching lipreading. She constructed a set of thirty training films at the Ohio State University for acoustically handicapped adults, and she also began a series of teaching films for young children. She prepared a manual to aid the instructor using the films, but her death occurred before the manual was published. The films provided supplementary material for the teacher and were not meant to replace him completely. She called her method Visual Hearing.[26]

Morkovin and Moore,[27] of the University of Southern California, also advocated the film approach in training. They too constructed films and wrote an accompanying manual for the teacher. Their films give the lipreader the opportunity to lipread persons in a variety of life situations—at the bank, at the dinner table, in the park, and so on.

A more detailed account of the methods of Bruhn, Nitchie, the Kinzies, Brauckmann, Mason, Morkovin, and Moore is given in following chapters which pertain specifically to methodology.

Present Status of Lipreading

Today in many institutions of higher learning throughout America, lipreading is offered to students of speech and hearing therapy, and

---

[25] Anna M. Bunger, *Speech Reading—Jena Method* (Danville, Illinois: The Interstate Press, 1944), pp. 13-15.

[26] Marie K. Mason, "A Cinematographic Technique For Testing More Objectively the Visual Speech Comprehension of Young Deaf and Hard of Hearing Children (Doctoral Dissertation, The Ohio State University Department of Speech, 1942).

[27] B. V. Morkovin and Lucelia M. Moore, *A Contextual Systematic Approach for Speech Reading* (Los Angeles: University of Southern California, 1948-49).

to prospective teachers of the deaf; today in many colleges, public and private elementary schools and high schools, as well as hospital clinics and hearing societies, lipreading is offered as a rehabilitative measure for the acoustically handicapped; and since the end of World War II, more attention has been given to lipreading as an aural rehabilitative measure for handicapped veterans. General Hospitals and Veteran's Administration training centers continue programs of lipreading instruction. Thus, today, lipreading has been brought to the attention of the general public, and has found its place with the other clinical and academic methods directed toward the education of the aurally handicapped.

It is clear that through the years many thousands of people have profited by their training in lipreading, but much remains to be discovered about lipreading itself. Currently, scientific research, directed toward the measurement of factors correlating with a person's ability or lack of ability to lipread, is being carried out in several colleges and clinics in the United States.

3

A LIPREADING TEST IS A SPECIALIZED EDUCATIONAL INSTRU-
ment, designed to measure a viewer's ability to understand what a speaker is saying by concentrating on his
lip movements and other facial muscles. As is the case
with other educational tests, it provides a means of
quantifying an aspect of human behavior.

There are several reasons why lipreading tests are
desirable. As previously mentioned, they can be used to
measure the basic lipreading ability of an individual.
The authors have seen young children with no formal
training lipreading better than some college adults who
have practiced for several months. Tests have shown
average students with greater lipreading ability than
superior students. The ability to lipread, however, is
not related to low scholastic achievement, for there are
also poor scholastic performers who are poor lipreaders,
and excellent lipreaders who excel in their studies. A
second reason that lipreading tests are desirable is that

TESTS OF LIPREADING

they can be employed to measure the effects of lipreading training. Although one cannot be certain of the factors that cause improvement in lipreading, many persons tend to increase their ability during practice. For example, in a study carried out by Oyer,[1] there was highly significant improvement in test scores made by a college class after they had observed eighteen hours of lipreading programs on television.

A third reason for the use of a lipreading test is to aid in the proper placement of individuals within a training program. For diagnostic purposes, it is necessary to sort out the acoustically handicapped who are excellent, average, and poor lipreaders. It is important for the clinician to know the lipreading status of his students, for then the lessons can be structured accordingly, and a decision made regarding the amount of specific lipreading training to be given in the overall rehabilitation program. Fourth, a lipreading test is helpful in deciding which teaching methods, or combination of methods, are most appropriate for students of various ages and performance levels. If the Bruhn, Jena, Kinzie and Nitchie methods, or variations thereof, are used, then the therapist seeking the best method, must discover from research and experience, which ones are most suitable for use with the acoustically handicapped of various ages and levels of lipreading proficiency. To determine the efficacy of a method, or to obtain comparisons between or among methods, testing before and after the approach is applied is mandatory. A valid and reliable test of lipreading is also a useful research tool. The literature provides information concerning whether I.Q., memory span, or other such phenomena relate meaningfully to an individual's ability to lipread.

Tests of lipreading need not only be instruments that measure the skill of a lipreader, they can also vindicate the visual intelligibility of individual speakers. In other words, they can point out persons who are either easy or difficult to lipread. Clinical experience shows that some people are much more difficult to lipread than others. Mouth opening, lip movements, eye movements, and other gestures and postures contribute to the ease or difficulty with which it can be done.

[1] H. J. Oyer, "Quantitative Assessment of Improvement in Lipreading Performance of Subjects Taught Via Closed Circuit Television" (accepted for publication by *Volta Review*, 1961).

Review of Formal Lipreading Tests

It is well for the reader to bear in mind that the following work represents the best in formal materials available at the present time. Although these tools are far from adequate, the practice of lipreading must continue, for regardless of our inabilities, many hard of hearing and deaf persons are gaining great proficiency in lipreading skills.

Stephens[2] points out that tests of lipreading skill can be classified under two types. The first is the face to face test, the second the silent motion picture film test. As early as 1913, E. B. Nitchie[3] attempted to assess the lipreading skill of the aurally handicapped by constructing a filmed lipreading test in which three proverbs were spoken— (1) "Tis love that makes the world go round," (2) "Spare the rod and spoil the child," and (3) "Fine feathers make fine birds." They were spoken at 11-12 movements per second, and photographed with a camera that operated at a speed of 16 frames per second. In his description of this brief test, Nitchie does not mention administering it to subjects; he does, however, present individual pictures of the sounds in the *Volta Review* article.

Two years later, Kitson[4] reported an investigation carried out to examine certain factors assumed to be related to lipreading ability. He constructed no formal tests, but used as a criterion measure lipreading aptitude as judged by teachers. His testing was done in face to face manner. A more detailed account of his study is presented in Chapter 4.

In 1917 Conklin[5] constructed a standardized lipreading test which utilized an objective scoring method. The test was of the face to face type, and the materials consisted of eight consonants, fifty-two words, and twenty sentences. Adolescent students at the Oregon State School for the Deaf were the subjects. They were provided with a prepared test form and wrote down what they thought had been spoken to them. For each consonant correctly identified, one point was given.

[2] M. C. Stephens, "An Experimental Investigation of the Relationship Among Three Filmed Lipreading Tests and Their Relationship to Teacher Ratings" (Master's Thesis, The Ohio State University Department of Speech, 1956).

[3] E. B. Nitchie, "Moving Pictures Applied to Lipreading," *The Volta Review*, 15 (1913), pp. 117-125.

[4] M. D. Kitson, "Psychological Tests for Lip Reading Ability," *The Volta Review*, 17 (1951), pp. 471-476.

[5] E. S. Conklin, "A Method for the Determination of Relative Skill in Lip-Reading," *The Volta Review*, 19 (1917), pp. 216-220.

For each word correctly read, one point was given, and for sentences, five points each were allowed. Analysis of the test scores revealed a high correlation (.90) between test scores and rankings assigned by the teachers, but analysis did not reveal any significant correlation between lipreading ability and chronological age.

Nitchie[6] commented upon the efficiency of the Conklin test and stated that the results achieved by the deaf subjects would not necessarily be expected from partially handicapped subjects because of the prevailing differences in language development between these two groups. He felt that the construction of a standardized test for general lipreading ability was not feasible. Nevertheless, the Conklin attempt helped stimulate general interest in lipreading tests. Wright[7] suggested that Conklin film his test so that teachers throughout the country could administer it, and thus establish some idea of its validity. This, however, was not accomplished. Bruhn,[8] in comparing the Conklin test with fifty syllables and twenty sentences from the Mueller-Walle materials, found that students showed a superior performance on the latter.

In 1928, Day and Fusfeld[9] constructed two lipreading tests and administered them face to face to 8,300 deaf pupils. Test materials consisted of four sets of ten sentences each. The test sentences were read to the pupils, who in turn were instructed to write down exactly what they read from the lips. One set was read by the teacher and the other by the field agent. Pintner's analysis showed that the speech reading scores achieved when the teachers read the lists were considerably higher than those achieved when the field agent read them. Pintner[10] stated that this was one of the first objective attempts at measuring the lipreading skill among the deaf. An analysis of the relationships of the speech reading tests, the Pintner Educational Survey Test, and the Pintner Nonlanguage Test, all given to the 8300 deaf pupils, is presented in Chapter 4.

In 1940, Heider and Heider[11] constructed three filmed tests of

[6] E. B. Nitchie, "Tests for Determining Skill in Lip-Reading," *The Volta Review*, 19 (1917), pp. 222-223.

[7] J. D. Wright, "Familiarity With Language the Prime Factor," *The Volta Review*, 19 (1917), pp, 223-224.

[8] M. E. Bruhn, "Relative Skill in Lipreading," *The Volta Review*, 19 (1917), pp. 220-222.

[9] H. E. Day, I. S. Fusefeld, and R. Pintner, *A Survey of American Schools for the Deaf: 1924-25* (Washington, D.C.: National Research Council, 1928).

[10] R. Pintner, "Speech and Speech Reading Tests For The Deaf," *Journal of Applied Psychology*, 13 (1929), 221.

[11] F. K. Heider and G. M. Heider, "Studies in the Psychology of the Deaf," *Psychological Monographs*, 52 (1940), pp. 124-133.

lipreading ability. Their purpose was to measure achievement among pupils at the Clarke School for the Deaf. The first test contained fifteen unrelated nouns, fifteen meaningless phonetic units, fifteen names of animals, fifteen unrelated sentences, and ten related sentences. The second test was comprised of thirty names of animals, thirty unrelated nouns, thirty unrelated sentences, and two stories, each containing approximately 150 words. The third test was the same as the second, except that the names of the animals were eliminated. The conclusions reached were that recognition of vowels was superior to consonant recognition, and that no correlation existed between the ability to lipread nonsense syllables and general lipreading ability.

In 1942 Mason[12] constructed a filmed lipreading test for children which could be scored objectively. First she constructed two exploratory tests that were designed to evaluate the lipreading skill of young acoustically handicapped children. Materials included:

> *Test I*
>   Form A: flower, cow, top, ball, fish
>   Form B: baby, car, cat, cup, shoe
> *Test II*
>   Form A: woman, boat, fork, man, comb, dog, boy, table, chair, girl
>   Form B: sheep, cap, book, muff, spoon, coat, knife, glove, glass, horse

Test I was to determine a pre-school deaf child's ability to recognize the visible kinaesthetic speech pattern set up as the words are spoken, and to translate into verbal concepts these visible movements. Test II, which included ten nouns of increasing visible difficulty, was supposed to measure achievement of a higher level. Not completely satisfied, Mason revised the test for children. Test III included all of the items of Tests I and II. In addition, fifteen new nouns were included. The selection of the test items conformed to specific criteria:

1. Their occurrence in the first three thousand of Thorndike's word frequency list.
2. Their place in building vocabulary for language comprehension of young deaf children in the early grades of schools for the deaf, and in classes for hypacusics.

[12] M. K. Mason, "A Cinematographic Technique For Testing More Objectively the Visual Speech Comprehension of Young Deaf and Hard of Hearing Children" (Doctoral Dissertation, The Ohio State University Department of Speech, 1942).

3. Their inclusion of the most frequently occurring consonant and vowel sounds.
4. The photogenic qualities of the concrete objects which symbolize the verbal concepts.
5. The freedom of the test words from visual ambiguity of meaning.
6. The distinct visible speech manifestations of the phonetic elements of which the test nouns are composed.
7. The lack of homophenity (visible similarity) in test words, except where deliberately planned, so as to test superior visual discrimination.
8. Their place in the life experiences of children, through toys, pictures, or actual objects.

The following words were included in Test III, Forms A and B:

Form A:
top, cow, ball, flower, fish, nose, orange, thumb, box, candy, ear, boat, comb, woman, dog, man, chair, fork, boy, table, girl, finger, key, bottle, cracker, bathtub, slipper, hairbrush, sweater, birdcage

Form B:
baby, arm, shoe, car, eye, cup, mouth, cat, flag, soap, sheep, horse, cap, book, coat, banana, glass, spoon, muff, pencil, knife, watch, cookie, towel, glove, stocking, basket, toothbrush, umbrella, rabbit.

This test was administered to 138 deaf children whose ages ranged from six to ten. A high correlation (.95) was found between the forms of the test.[13] The Mason test for children is illustrated in Appendix A.

Pauls,[14] in 1945, described how she utilized Naval Training films, and selected and edited commercial shorts from featured motion picture films as informal tests by which she could measure a veteran's progress in lipreading. These were employed also as training aids.

In a speech given in 1946 at the summer meeting of the American Association To Promote the Teaching of Speech to The Deaf, Utley[15] described the development and standardization procedures she used in her motion picture achievement tests of lipreading ability. The test consisted of words, sentences, and stories. The words were taken from the Thorndike list of most frequently used words and the sentences were composed of trial statements, common expressions, and idiomatic expressions. Utley administered the test,

---

[13] M. K. Mason, "A Cinematographic Technique For Testing Visual Speech Comprehension," *Journal of Speech Disorders*, 8 (1943), pp. 271-278.

[14] Miriam Pauls, "Speech Reading," *Hearing and Deafness*, edited by Hallowell Davis (New York: Murray Hill Books, Inc., 1947), p. 269.

[15] J. Utley, "Factors Involved In the Teaching And Testing of Lipreading Ability Through The Use of Motion Pictures," *The Volta Review*, (1946), pp. 657-659.

without voice, to 200 subjects of different grade levels who had
normal hearing. Subsequently, after analyzing her results, she revised
her test, filmed it, and administered it to 100 students in two schools
for the deaf. The Sentence and Word Tests were presented by a
university coed and were photographed on black-and-white film,
while the Story Test was filmed in color. In this latter section a
small boy, a man, and two women presented the materials. Fifteen
seconds were allowed for pupils to respond in writing to the sentences and questions, and ten seconds elapsed between words. Blank
film was spliced into the test to allow for writing time. The complete
film was entitled, "How Well Can You Read Lips?" Utley's conclusions determined that there was interrelation among the skills of
word, sentence and story recognition. In addition, she stated that
the ability to lipread sentences was more reliably predicted from
an ability to lipread stories than words, but, the ability to lipread
words was more reliably predicted from an ability to lipread sentences than stories. Moreover, the ability to lipread stories was more
reliably predicted from an ability to lipread sentences than words.
Other interesting conclusions are given in more detail in the chapter
on research.

In 1947, Reid [16] reported preliminary work done on the construction and administration of a test in lipreading. This test
was filmed, and had three forms with five parts to each form. The
parts were comprised of 17 vowels and diphthongs, 11 consonants,
ten unrelated sentences, related sentences which told a story, and
also a short story. The story was followed by four questions. Three
different speakers, differing in educational and speech backgrounds,
were photographically reproduced on each of the forms. All three
forms were given to 99 girls enrolled in schools for the deaf. Inter-
form correlation was high (.83), thus indicating that there was apparently little relationship between the speakers' speech backgrounds or
accents and the ability of the subjects to read his lips.

The same year Morkovin[17] reported on the development of a
series of ten films designed as training materials for the acoustically
handicapped. The films were built around everyday experiences.
Following each film were questions to be answered by the lipreader.

---

[16] G. Reid, "A Preliminary Investigation In the Testing of Lipreading Achievement,"
Journal of Speech Disorders, 12 (1947), pp. 77-82.

[17]. B. V. Morkovin, "Rehabilitation of the Aurally Handicapped Through The Study
of Speech Reading In Life Situations," *Journal of Speech Disorders*, 12 (1947), pp.
363-368.

In a sense, this too was a test of lipreading ability, but as yet little information has been gathered regarding the use of the Morkovin-Moore films as a direct lipreading test. DiCarlo and Kataja[18] utilized the second film of the series, "The Family Dinner," to establish the validity of the Utley Test. A high correlation (.77) was obtained between scores achieved on the two films by aurally handicapped subjects. Stephens[19] later compared the Mason ($\#30$), Utley (Form A) and Morkovin-Moore ($\#101$) films in an attempt to determine the adequacy of each one. She found that the Mason Test Film ($\#30$) correlated significantly with the Utley (Form A) and the Morkovin-Moore film ($\#101$). The Utley (Form A), however, did not correlate with the Morkovin-Moore film ($\#101$). Even though the Morkovin-Moore film ($\#101$) was not designed as a testing instrument, it appears, however, that it can be used as such.

In 1949, Cavender[20] explored the relationship of lipreading skill to other factors related to the lipreading situation. She constructed a sentence test, including words which were determined to be within the reading vocabulary of the first three grades. Her test was administered in a face to face manner, because she felt it gave a more normal testing situation, since the viewing was three dimensional, the lighting similar to that encountered in the classroom, and no equipment was required. In addition, she felt that better attention and rapport could be established with face to face, rather than filmed, testing. Upon administering her test to 180 persons, some of whom were acoustically handicapped, Cavender concluded that it was not feasible to argue against film type tests, for they proved to be as consistent in their results as face-to-face ones.

Kelly,[21] in developing a test of lipreading ability, to be used for either face to face or filmed presentation, employed lists of letters, multiple-choice word lists, and sentences. Section I of the Kelly test consisted of fifteen three letter items, that is, (1) AIE; (2) YBU; (3) IGM; and so on. Section II, labeled "Words Out of Context," was composed of ten items—such as:

[18] L. DiCarlo and R. Kataja, "An Analysis of the Utley Lipreading Test," *Journal of Speech and Hearing Disorders*, 16 (1951), pp. 226-240.

[19] M. C. Stephens, "An Experimental Investigation of the Relationship Among Three Filmed Lipreading Tests and Their Relationship to Teacher Ratings" (Master's Thesis, The Ohio State University Department of Speech, 1956).

[20] B. J. Cavender, "The Construction and Investigation Of a Test of Lip Reading Ability and a Study of Factors Assumed To Affect The Results" (Master's Thesis, Indiana University Department of Speech, 1949).

[21] J. C. Kelly, "Audio-Visual Speech Reading" (University of Illinois, 1955), 39 pp. (Mimeographed).

(1) Number one is	whisper	shoe
(2) Number two is	window	baseball
(3) Number three is	picture	fish

After number five, three alternatives were presented for selection. The third section of the test was comprised of ten sentences, three of which were questions. There were four three-word sentences, four four-word sentences, and two with five words each. The following are examples: (1) Thank you very much. (3) What is your name? (6) We like baseball. Test-retest correlation on his materials was found to be quite high (.86).

Lowell,[22] in 1957, reported research on a filmed lipreading test constructed at the John Tracy Clinic. The test, entitled *Film Test of Lip Reading,* consisted of sixty unrelated sentences which were simple in content, and might well have occurred in everyday conversation. Examples included: "Did you get my letter?"—"I'll meet you at three o'clock." The sentences were selected from research films originally prepared by the Department of Otolaryngology, State University of Iowa.

The *Film Test of Lip Reading* was administered to 408 college students with normal hearing. Results were statistically analyzed to determine reliability, and analysis revealed that half of the test, 30 sentences, was just as reliable as the entire 60 sentences. Therefore two forms, Form A and B were constructed. These were subsequently tested with 173 college students with normal hearing and the mean score difference between them was not found to be significant.

Moser and colleagues,[23] in 1960, constructed a filmed test of visual recognition with one-syllable words. The stimuli were taken from Voelker's[24] list of the 1,000 most frequently spoken words. Four speakers were filmed saying the words. Analysis showed the test to be reliable, but future research will determine how well its results correlate with results of a test using sentences.

Informal Assessment of Lipreading Ability

It is not always practical, nor is it always feasible to administer a formal lipreading test when first determining a person's lipreading

[22] E. L. Lowell, "A Film Test of Lip Reading," John Tracy Research Papers II, John Tracy Clinic. (Los Angeles, California, November 1957).

[23] H. M. Moser, H. J. Oyer, J. J. O'Neill, and H. J. Gardner, *Selection of Items For Testing Skill in Visual Recognition of One-Syllable Words* (The Ohio State University Development Fund Project Number 5818, 1960).

[24] Charles H. Voelker, "The One-Thousand Most Frequent Spoken-Words," *Quarterly Journal of Speech,* 28 (1942), pp. 189-197.

skill. Often in the initial interview with an acoustically handicapped person, the interviewer will attempt to discover to what extent a patient is relying upon lipreading as a supplement to his auditory cues. Sometimes it is obvious that the patient is watching every move of the examiner's lips. Continuing the conversation at the same vocal level, but covering the lips with a piece of paper or the hand, often proves disconcerting to the person who really depends upon lipreading for understanding. It is interesting to note the effort made by some malingerers to impress an examiner with their dependence upon lipreading. However, they betray themselves by concentrating on the eyes, not the lips, of the tester.

Recently one of the authors had occasion to test the hearing of a six year old child who was severely handicapped. As the stimulus words (which were names of toys) were delivered to her from the control room via phones, she struggled hard to select the proper toys. She had little success until the auditory stimuli were supplemented with visual stimuli from the lips of the tester. Her correct identification score then rose from almost zero to 80-85 per cent. Although a formal test was not administered, the examiner was able to see that the youngster was a proficient lipreader.

For those hard of hearing who rely upon auditory cues, one may use diminished voice in asking questions to determine how well they can lipread. The questions should be simple and of the type occurring in daily conversation. For example, "How old are you?"—"Where do you live?"—"Do you have a car?"

In testing small children, it is best to employ informal methods involving the use of simple commands, playing games with blocks, or identification of pictures and objects. The success of any method with a young child depends upon the examiner's ability to establish adequate rapport. Some examiners can deal with youngsters easily, whereas others, no matter how hard they try, seem doomed to failure. Minski[25] implies that some deaf children under the age of two years can learn to lipread. If one were to test informally a child so young, the vocabulary used would have to be highly selective. Minski suggests a test of calling for the child to repeat unfamiliar syllables as he hears and sees them spoken by the examiner. The child's back is then turned toward the examiner as the syllables are spoken to see whether he can repeat them again without visual cues.

Precise judgments, however, cannot be made on the basis of

[25] Louis Minski, *Deafness, Mutism, and Mental Deficiency In Children* (New York: Philosophical Library, 1957), p. 1.

informal testing procedures. Even though we read the same words, phrases, or sentences to the subjects, it is almost impossible to duplicate the same testing conditions. Light in the room, arrangement of the objects in the room, angle at which the subject reads, lip and facial movements made by the tester in reproducing the stimuli, and other variables contribute to inaccuracy when using informal face to face testing. Informal procedures, however, are valuable in situations where a precise determination of ability is not mandatory, or in instances where no retesting will be done.

Factors to Consider in Constructing a Test of Lipreading

In constructing a measuring instrument, specific steps must be taken to make the instrument meaningful. In constructing a lipreading test as, in fact, in constructing *any* educational test, the same rules apply. *Valid* and *reliable* results must be forthcoming. The lipreading test must indicate the lipreading skill of the viewer, and, upon readministration, it must yield scores that correlate significantly with those obtained on the first testing.

The *ideal* or *perfect* test, of course, will probably exist only as a theoretical formulation, but the characteristics of the ideal test can serve as guides for the lipreading-test builder. Here are some of the main factors to be considered in designing such a test: (1) the population to be tested, (2) the general format of the test, (3) the selection of speakers, (4) the selection of test items, (5) conditions under which the test will be given, (6) the scoring procedures to be employed.

1. *The Population to Be Tested.* In planning the lipreading test, the constructor must decide for whom the test is to be built. If it is for children, their age levels, their degree of deafness, and their oral language background must be considered. If the test is for older children and adults, their educational background must also be considered as well as whether they were deaf from birth or from early years before they learned oral language, or whether they lost their hearing after developing oral language skills. In other words, age, experience backgrounds, and proficiency in oral language reception and expression are all important factors.

Ideally, the test should be appropriate for old and young alike; that is, age and experience should have no effects upon the likelihood of success or failure in the lipreading task. The test should also be appropriate for the uneducated. The test vocabulary should be carefully chosen so that those deficient in language background have an equal chance for successful performance with those rich in language background. The main task is to derive meaning from a speaker's lip and facial configurations, and the items of the test should measure the subject's performance of this task, not his formal education. Items from highly specialized or technical vocabularies, or words or expressions peculiar to religious and ethnic groups or geographical locations should not be included in the test.

2. *General Format of the Test.* The test constructor must determine the the exact format of his test. Most lipreading tests have been of the *write-down* type, although the reader may recall the Mason[26] multiple-choice test for children. In designing a multiple-choice test, the constructor should be aware that he is restricting the vocabulary from which his subjects can select their answers. If the items for selection are either obviously different or similar as far as the visual clues are concerned, it is clear that different degrees of perceptive skill are involved. Visually homophenous items create confusion, whereas words involving quite different lip and facial configurations are often too easy; thus the test fails to measure, with precision, real lipreading ability. Furthermore, if the answer sheet is of the multiple-choice type, the format must not influence the lipreader's responses. Systematic investigation of answer sheets has shown that their construction may significantly affect a subject's response.[27] Such an investigation by Moser and the authors suggested that multiple-choice formats with less than three crossout items from which to choose resulted in a non-chance type distribution. In a multiple-choice test, the best number of items from which to choose an answer is between five and eight.

On the other hand, the write-down test calls for the selection of items from an almost limitless vocabulary. This type of test appears to come closer to being a true test of real lipreading ability. However, in real-life lipreading situations, the visual clues are selected from a restricted vocabulary that is often quite limited by context.

3. *Selection of Speakers.* As mentioned before, some persons are much easier to lipread than others. The same is true in intelligibility testing involving auditory clues. Therefore, in building a test that

[26] M. K. Mason, Doctoral Dissertation, Ohio State University (1942). See Appendix A, page 141.

[27] H. M. Moser, J. J. O'Neill, and H. J. Oyer, "Effect of Test Format on Listener Response," *Central States Speech Journal,* 10 (Spring 1959), pp. 39-47.

represents the lipreading task fairly, speakers of varying degrees of lipreadability should be included.

Speakers also should represent race, dialect, sex, and age in proportion to the frequency of their occurrence in the over-all population of a country. These factors should then be represented in proportion to the frequency of their occurrence in the population for which the test is built. Great care must be exercised in making random selection of the speakers within the racial, dialectal, age, and sex categories set up.

4. *Selection of Test Items.* Included in the test could be one or several different items such as a series of isolated sounds, syllables, words, or sentences. In the event a series of isolated sounds is used, the sounds must be selected with reference to specific criteria: the frequency of their occurrence in the language, and the visibility of each of the sounds. Test items also should be equally familiar to all who take the test. Information relating to word familiarity can be found in the following sources:

(a) Black, J. W. and Marian Ausherman, *The Vocabulary Of College Students in Classroom Speeches.* Columbus, Ohio: Bureau of Educational Research, The Ohio State University, 1955.

(b) Dale, Edgar, *Bibliography of Vocabulary Studies.* Columbus, Ohio: Bureau of Educational Research, The Ohio State University, 1949.

(c) Dewey, Godfrey, *The Relative Frequency of English Speech Sounds.* Cambridge, Mass: Harvard University Press, 1923.

(d) Fossum, Ernest C., "An Analysis of the Dynamic Vocabulary of Junior College Students," *Speech Monographs,* 11 (1944), pp. 88-96.

(e) Fraprie, Frank R., "The Twenty Commonest English Words . . . From a Count of 242,432 Words of English Text Taken From Fifteen English Authors and Many Newspapers," in *World Almanac and Book of Facts for 1950,* ed. Harvey Hansen. New York: World-Telegram, p. 543.

(f) French, Norman R., Charles W. Carter, Jr., and Walter Koenig, Jr., "The Words and Sounds of Telephone Conversation," *Bell System Technical Journal,* 9 (April, 1930), pp. 290-324.

(g) Horn, Ernest H., *Basic Writing Vocabulary: 10,000 Words Most Commonly Used in Writing.* Iowa City, Iowa: College of Education, University of Iowa, 1926. University of Iowa Monographs in Education, First Series, No. 4.

(h) Thorndike, E. L. and Irving Lorge, *The Teacher's Word Book of 30,000 Words.* New York: Bureau of Publications, Teachers College, Columbia University, 1944.

(i) Voelker, Charles H., "The One-Thousand Most Frequent Spoken-Words," *Quarterly Journal of Speech,* 28 (1942), pp. 189-197.

After items for the test have been tentatively selected, they must be tried out in order to eliminate those proving to be unsatisfactory. Conrad [28] suggested that the experimental selection of test items was comprised of three stages: the pre-tryout, the tryout proper, and the final test administration. In item selection, the test constructor must utilize stimuli that will contribute most toward effective measurement. In other words, the test items must not be so difficult that all examinees miss them, nor so easy that the examinees get them all correct.

5. *Test Conditions.* In administering a lipreading test, the test conditions should be carefully controlled. Among the variables to consider in a filmed test, for example, are the size of the image on the screen, clarity of focus, projector speed, light in the test environment, angle and distance at which the screen image is viewed, the time length of exposure of the image, and the time interval between stimuli presentation.

6. *Scoring Procedure.* It is advisable for the constructor to decide upon the scoring procedure before selecting items for the test. There would be a difference in the stimuli selected if the scores were based upon correct identification of sounds, syllables, and words than if they were based upon meanings. Remember that the real reason for lipreading, just as for hearing, is for one person to know what another person has said. Specific numeral values also should be assigned to the items that are employed so that the performance of the persons tested can be mathematically summarized.

Ideally, test forms should be of the self-scoring type. Those who have worked hard and long scoring tests can best appreciate this suggestion. With very little expense and effort, the test form, if of the multiple-choice type, can be set up so that the subject's response is impressed on a second sheet by means of a throw-away carbon that lies between.

Summary

A lipreading test is constructed in order to determine how well one person can tell what another is saying by reading his lips. Some per-

---

[28] Herbert S. Conrad, "The Experimental Tryout of Test Materials," from *Educational Measurement,* E. F. Lindquist, ed. (Menasha, Wisc.: American Council on Education, George Banta Publishing Company, 1951), pp. 251 ff.

sons are more easily lipread than others. For many years attempts have been made to construct tests of lipreading ability. Some have been face to face tests and others filmed. Only a few skills have been found to correlate with the ability to lipread. It is possible to make informal assessment of a person's ability to lipread. This is done when time or other factors do not permit administering a formal test. Some factors to consider in constructing an ideal test of lipreading are the population for whom the test is designed, the format of the test, the speakers, test items, testing conditions, and scoring procedures.

4

A LOGICAL WAY TO APPROACH THE PROBLEM OF THE EX-
perimental study of lipreading is to outline the variables present in the usual lipreading situation. The
schematic depicted in Figure 3 presents a listing of the
possible variables that might be considered in any experimental study of the lipreading process.

SPEAKER-SENDER	LIPREADER-RECEIVER
1. Facial characteristics	1. Visual acuity and discrimination
2. Articulatory movements	2. Communication "set"
(a) Rate of speaking	3. Residual hearing
(b) Distinctness of speaking	4. Personality
3. Gesture activity	(a) Intelligence
4. Amount of voice used	(b) Behavior patterns
5. Feedback characteristics	(c) Past communicative experience
	(d) Visual feedback
ENVIRONMENT	CODE OR STIMULUS
1. Lighting conditions	1. Visibility
2. Physical arrangements	2. Familiarity
3. Number of senders	3. Structure
4. Physical distractions	4. Rate of transmission
	5. Auditory-visual aspects

FIGURE 3. *Schematic of variables involved in the lipreading process.*

THE EXPERIMENTAL STUDY OF LIPREADING

It is realized that there can be variations of this arrangement. For example, if two aurally handicapped persons are speaking to each other the following type of arrangement might hold:

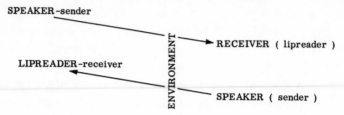

FIGURE 4. *Representation of communication between two hard-of-hearing individuals.*

In this instance it would be interesting to determine if difficulty with the lipreading of a speaker would have an effect on the articulatory activities of the other hard of hearing member of the speaker-receiver team. Would he tend to exaggerate his lip movements? Would he tend to simplify the message he is trying to get across?

The research discussed in the present chapter deals with the attributes of the lipreader and the effects of environment, type of stimuli, and character of the speaker upon lipreading performance. It is necessary to remember that there is another research aspect to lipreading; the construction of tests of lipreading ability. This material has been discussed in Chapter 3.

However, it will be necessary to include the tests with the materials discussed in this chapter, for the lipreading skill of an individual must, of necessity, be determined by means of standardized tests. As a result, an uncontrolled variable may be introduced into the testing situation as the majority of lipreading tests have not been validated. Thus, the type of lipreading test will be responsible for the categorizing of test subjects. Since there is not a true measure of lipreading ability, only a relative one, this may lead to experimental results that will be difficult to explain.

The first experimental investigation of lipreading was attempted in 1914 by Kitson.[1] His research involved a study of the various factors assumed to be related to lipreading skill. Since that time there have been scattered experimental studies. In the early 1950's, Ohio State University began a series of studies aimed at the evaluation of

[1] H. D. Kitson, "Psychological Tests for Lipreading Ability," *The Volta Review*, 17 (1915), pp. 471-476.

the skills possessed by lipreaders. In the mid-1950's, the John Tracy Clinic began a program of research under a grant from the Office of Vocational Rehabilitation. This program has resulted in the publication of a series of research papers.

In the area of lipreading that relates to the lipreader, the majority of research has been confined to three basic areas—intelligence, behavioral patterns and visual skills. This research has involved the testing of the lipreading skills of normal hearing, hard of hearing and deaf individuals. For the sake of convenience, the results of this research will be reported under four categories—the lipreader or perceiver, the environment, the stimulus materials, and the speaker or sender. Only the exclusive results of the specific skills under study will be discussed. However, overlapping will occur because certain investigations involved the study of several attributes at one time. One final area will deal with research that does not directly fit under the four main categories.

The Lipreader or Receiver

In studying the behavior of the lipreader, three areas of research interest are involved—intelligence, personality, and visual skill. The discussion will begin with an account of the research dealing with the relationship between intelligence and lipreading ability.

Intelligence

In the early 1900's, the majority of men studying human behavior became convinced that the criterion for all behavior was intelligence. The earliest studies of skills associated with lipreading ability centered around possible relationships between such an ability and intelligence. Kitson[2] completed a study involving the presentation of tachistoscopic materials, reading tests and a completion test. The results of these tests were compared to the results obtained on a specially constructed face to face lipreading test. A conventional intelligence test was not used, but a completion test which served as a rough measure of *syntheticability* was employed. As was the habit of early researchers, correlations were mentioned with little discussion of their significance. The results could be said to indicate that subjects who had high scores in visual skills also rated high on lipreading tests. It was assumed from these results that the good lipreader had a large visual span and was a good guesser.

[2] Kitson, *ibid.*

Pintner,[3] in 1929, employed face to face lipreading tests in a study of the lipreading ability of deaf students enrolled in a residential school. These tests had been originally developed by Day, Fusfeld and Pintner for use in a survey of the lipreading ability of deaf students enrolled in residential schools. The results of Pintner's studies indicated that there was no significant correlation between lipreading ability and scores obtained on the Pintner Non-Language Mental Test. The Heiders,[4] using a personally developed filmed test of lipreading performance, surveyed the lipreading ability of students enrolled at the Clarke School. They found no significant relationship between lipreading proficiency and school achievement. Reid,[5] also using a filmed lipreading test which was administered to 99 girls enrolled in schools for the deaf, found that there was no significant correlation between scores obtained on the test and scholastic achievement and intelligence (Stanford Achievement Tests).

Several studies have been conducted in which the lipreading ability of normal hearing subjects was compared with their performance on intelligence tests. In 1949, Cavender,[6] using a face to face test and a population of normal hearing children in the sixth, ninth and twelfth grades, reported that there was no significant relationship between intelligence scores and the scores obtained on the lipreading test. The intelligence scores were obtained from the school files. O'Neill[7] used one of the Mason filmed lipreading tests in a study of factors associated with skill in lipreading. The results of the study, involving normal hearing college students, indicated that only two of the 27 skills that were evaluated correlated significantly with lipreading ability. One of these skills was performance intelligence as measured by the Wechsler-Bellevue Adult Intelligence Scale. In a continuation of this study, O'Neill and Davidson[8] investigated the relationship between lipreading ability and intelligence as measured

[3] R. Pintner, "Speech and Speech Reading Tests for the Deaf," *Journal of Applied Psychology*, 12 (1929), pp. 220-225.

[4] F. Heider and G. Heider, "An Experimental Investigation of Lip Reading," *Psychological Monographs*, 52 (1), (1940), pp. 1-153.

[5] Gladys Reid, "A Preliminary Investigation in the Test of Lipreading Achievement," *American Annals of the Deaf*, 91 (1946), pp. 403-413.

[6] Betty J. Cavender, "The Construction and Investigation of a Test of Lip Reading Ability and a Study of Factors Assumed to Affect the Results" (Master's Thesis, Indiana University Department of Speech, 1949).

[7] John J. O'Neill, "An Exploratory Investigation of Lipreading Ability Among Normal Hearing Students," *Speech Monographs*, 18 (1951), pp. 309-311.

[8] John J. O'Neill and J. L. Davidson, "Relationship Between Lipreading Ability and Five Psychological Factors," *Journal of Speech and Hearing Disorders*, 21 (1956), pp. 478-481.

by the Ohio State Psychological Examination. (This test is used as the entrance examination at Ohio State University, and the results are reported in terms of percentiles or relationship to a standardization group.) The results of the comparisons indicated that there was no significant relationship between lipreading skill and intelligence. The adult form of the Wechsler-Bellevue scale was also used by Simmons[9] in a study involving 24 hard of hearing subjects. No significant correlation was found between intelligence quotients obtained on the Wechsler-Bellevue test and three measures of lipreading ability.

The results of the above studies conclude that there is no definite established relationship between lipreading ability and intelligence as measured by a variety of tests.

Behavioral Patterns

Of particular interest to teachers of lipreading, as well as to research workers in the area, is a study of the behavioral patterns possessed by individuals who exhibit proficiency in lipreading. In the discussion to follow, behavior will be considered in very broad terms. Stobschinski[10] discussed the potential behavior of a lipreader in terms of types of thought processes that might be used. He indicated that the process of lipreading should be considered as a form of *speech thinking*. There are four types of speech thinking: the visual, the acoustic, the speech-motor and script-motor type of thought. He further stated that the individual with the visual type of thought would be best suited to lipreading, with the motor type being next in line of adaptability. Stobschinski felt that the person who utilized the acoustic type of thought would have the greatest difficulties with lipreading. One of the first experimental studies of the behavior patterns of speech readers was undertaken by O'Neill [11] who administered a battery of tests to a group of normal hearing college students with varying degrees of lipreading skill. Included among the tests were the Rotter Incomplete Sentence Test, the Rorschach Test, the Knower Speech Attitude Scale and the Knower-Dusenbury

---

[9] Audrey A. Simmons, "Factors Related to Lipreading," *Journal of Speech and Hearing Research*, 2 (1959), pp. 340-352.

[10] Robert Stobschinski, "Lip Reading: Its Psychological Aspects and Its Adaptation to the Individual Needs of the Hard of Hearing," *American Annals of the Deaf*, 73 (1928), pp. 234-242.

[11] *Speech Monographs*, 18, *op. cit.*

Test of Ability to Judge Emotions. The results of the study indicated that there were no significant relationships between the areas of behavior sampled by the various tests and skill in lipreading. Thus, it appeared that orientation to speech, ability to judge emotions, and the results of projective tests of personality did not relate to lipreading ability. A similar experimental group of subjects was utilized by O'Neill and Davidson[12] in an investigation of level of aspiration behavior and lipreading skill. No significant relationship was found to exist between lipreading competence and level of aspiration behavior. In short, good and poor lipreaders did not differ in their reactions to success and failure.

The relationship between lipreading ability and certain personality factors among a population of congenitally deaf high school students was investigated by Worthington.[13] The Rotter Level of Aspiration Test, the Rotter Sentence Completion Test and the Mason filmed lipreading test were selected for study in the investigation. The results of the study indicated that there was no significant correlation between patterns of behavior or degrees of adjustment and lipreading ability. Wong and Taaffe[14] evaluated relationships obtained between aptitude and lipreading test performance and between personality and lipreading test performance. The Guilford-Zimmerman Temperament Survey was utilized in the measurement of ten personality variables. The Primary Mental Abilities Reasoning Test was also administered along with nine other aptitude tests. A population of normal hearing college students was used in the study. The results of the study indicated that general activity, personal relations and emotional instability were the personality dimensions important in lipreading. Reasoning, ideational fluency, spontaneous flexibility, and associational fluency appeared to be the important aptitudes.

While it is true that the results of the studies discussed give some indications of possible relationships between lipreading skill and certain personality or behavioral factors, there are still no definite indications of what constitutes the typical behavior of a good lipreader. This is an area that requires further experimentation and

[12] O'Neill and Davidson, *op. cit.*

[13] A. M. Worthington, "An Investigation of the Relationship Between the Lipreading Ability of Congenitally Deaf High School Students and Certain Personality Factors" (Doctoral Dissertation, The Ohio State University Department of Speech, 1956).

[14] Wilson Wong and Gordon Taaffe, "Relationships Between Selected Aptitude and Personality Tests and Lipreading Ability," *John Tracy Clinic Research Papers*, VII (February 1958).

the use of more refined measuring instruments. It may even be necessary to resort to a phenomenological or perceptual evaluation of the behavior of the lipreader.

Visual Skills

This would appear to be an area which should have received extensive study. The earliest lipreading texts stressed the importance of eye training. Also, there is a wealth of equipment as well as extensive research experience in the area of evaluation of visual skills. Yet, there are only three or four studies which have concerned themselves with some evaluation of visual skills and lipreading performance. The first of these studies was undertaken by Kitson[15] who utilized tachistoscopic techniques to evaluate visual awareness and visual attention span. The results of the study indicated that subjects who had high scores in visual skills also rated high on lipreading tests. O'Neill[16] used the Case-Ruch test of Spatial Relations in an effort to evaluate one aspect of visual perception, while O'Neill and Davidson[17] utilized tachistoscopic recognition of digits. In neither instance was there any significant relationship between skill in these visual areas and proficiency in lipreading.

Another area of consideration is that of visual-motor co-ordination. (In other words, a more detailed study should be made of the role of visual organization in skill in lipreading. Several tests of visual-motor co-ordination were used by O'Neill and by O'Neill and Davidson.) These tests included tests of block design, object assembly, and digit symbol from the Wechsler-Bellevue Tests of Adult Intelligence, and the Hanfmann and Kasanin Test. The first of these studies found that a significant correlation existed between scores for Digit Symbol performance and lipreading performance. However, there was no significant relationship between lipreading ability and scores obtained on the block design and object assembly tests. Such results pose a question as to whether the ability to comprehend relationships (abstracting ability) should not be investigated further. The Hanfmann-Kasanin test was used in the second study. The results of the study showed that there was no significant relationship between lipreading ability and scores obtained on the Hanfmann-

---

[15] Kitson, *op. cit.*

[16] *Speech Monographs,* 18, *op cit.*

[17] O'Neill and Davidson, *op. cit.*

Kasanin test. This would seem to indicate that lipreading may involve, not the recognition of verbal elements, but the recognition of configurations or form patterns. Simmons[18] utilized the same tests in a study of twenty-four aurally handicapped persons who had not received any previous lipreading training. She reported a significant correlation between the scores obtained on the Digit Symbol, Picture Arrangement and Block Design sub-tests of the Wechsler-Bellevue test and two of three tests of lipreading performance. However, there was no significant relationship between the results obtained on the Hanfmann-Kasanin test and lipreading performance, as measured by three specific tests of lipreading.

One other area of interest deals with reading skill. The results of two studies[19,20] indicate that there was no apparent relationship between lipreading ability and reading comprehension and reading rate. Of five areas sampled in the Iowa Reading Test, Simmons[21] found that only one of the areas (ability to extract key words) correlated with lipreading performance as measured by two filmed tests of lipreading performance (Mason and Utley tests).

It appears that there is no definite relationship between lipreading ability and visual skill. However, indications show that further investigations of perceptual skills, that is, memory span, perceptual field, social consciousness and imagery types should be made. It would be interesting to determine whether the good lipreader is of the visual imagery type as opposed to the auditory, or motor-kinesthetic type.

Miscellaneous

An early study by Gault[22] explored a deaf subject's recognition of words by vision and also by vision plus tactual sense. The results indicated that about twice as many words were recognized by vision and touch, as were recognized by vision alone. In this study tactual stimulation was applied to the finger tips by means of the Teletactor.

Blakeley[23] attempted to determine whether the ability to interpret

[18] Simmons, *op. cit.*

[19] *Speech Monographs,* 18, *op. cit.*

[20] O'Neill and Davidson, *op. cit.*

[21] Simmons, *op. cit.*

[22] Robert Gault, "On the Identification of Certain Vowel and Consonant Elements in Words by Their Tactual Qualities and by Their Visual Qualities as Seen by Lipreading," *Journal of Abnormal Psychology,* 22 (1927-28), pp. 33-39.

[23] Robert W. Blakeley, "Auditory Abilities Associated With Lip Reading" (Master's Thesis, University of Oregon Department of Speech, 1953).

and synthesize visual cues into meaningful language, as in lipreading, was closely associated with corresponding abilities in interpreting incomplete patterns of speech. Normal hearing college students were given the Utley filmed test, a slow speech test (sentences recorded at 78 rpm played back at 40 rpm), an auditory memory span test, and an interrupted speech test (as sentences were being recorded 65 circuit breaks per minute were introduced). Comparisons were then made between performances on the various tests. No significant relationship was found between lipreading ability and between auditory memory span or ability to interpret incomplete patterns of speech. A pilot study conducted at the John Tracy Clinic compared the relationship between lipreading ability and the auditory reception of distorted or masked speech.[24] The results of the study indicated that while lipreading and listening to distorted speech were somewhat related, they were not related in a linear way. The demonstrated relationship suggested that the best and worst lipreaders were the poorer listeners, and the middle range lipreaders were the better listeners. As part of an extensive investigation of factors pertaining to lipreading skill, Simmons[25] reported a significant correlation between the duration of hearing loss, visual memory span, and lipreading proficiency, as measured by an interview type of test. The visual memory span involved a test of memory for pictured objects. In the instance of filmed lipreading tests (Mason and Utley films), there was a significant relationship between rhythm, synthetic ability and visual memory span. The Rhythm test of Part A of the Seashore Test of Musical Talent, a fragmentary sentences test, and the previously mentioned object span test were used to evaluate ability in the areas of rhythm, synthetic ability and visual memory.

The Environment

Very little research has been accomplished or projected in the area of the environment and its effects on lipreading. Indirectly, Mulligan[26] studied one aspect of this area when she investigated the effects distance and speed of projection had upon the viewing of a filmed test of lipreading. The results of the study indicated that the slower

---

[24] Edgar L. Lowell, "Pilot Studies in Lip Reading," *John Tracy Clinic Research Papers,* VIII (February, 1958).
[25] Simmons, *op. cit.*
[26] Marigene Mulligan, "Variables in the Reception of Visual Speech from Motion Pictures" (Master Thesis, Ohio State University Department of Speech, 1954).

speed of projection (16 frames per second as compared to 24 frames per second) resulted in more correct recognition of the filmed materials. The distance between the subjects and the screen did not significantly effect test results. However, of the four distances studied, 5, 10, 15 and 20 feet, ten feet was apparently the most favorable viewing distance. A limited evaluation of the effects of changes in the auditory environment was reported by Miller and others[27] who studied the consequences of delayed auditory feedback upon lipreading performance. The results of the investigation indicated that after subjects had been exposed to delayed sidetone of the order of .19 seconds, there was an increase in lipreading ability. It was postulated that the improvement in lipreading ability could be contributed to increased attention to tactile sensation or a sharpening of general attentiveness. Outside of these two studies, there are no others that deal with the effects of environment upon lipreading. Controlled studies should be made of the effects of lighting, physical environment, distractions, and viewing distance upon the lipreading responses of subjects. Research, however, may have been discouraged because of the difficulty of controlling the variables existing in such situations.

Code or Stimulus Materials

The difficulty of a stimulus, whether auditory or visual, is of interest to the experimenter. The responses of subjects can only be understood when the difficulty of the stimulus is understood. Studies of speech reception or intelligibility have made extensive use of stimulus materials in terms of their organization, their familiarity, their structure, and their temporal patterns. Very few such evaluations have been made of the difficulty of lipreading stimulus materials. Morris,[28] in 1944, investigated the effects of three aspects of stimulus materials upon lipreading performance—(a) the position of a sentence within a group, (b) the position of a group within a sequence of groups, and (c) the length of sentences. The materials were presented in a face to face testing situation to a group of deaf subjects. Results indicated that there was a definite decline in lipreading

[27] J. Miller, C. L. Rousey, and C. R. Goetzinger, "An Exploratory Investigation of a Method of Improving Speech Reading," *American Annals of the Deaf*, 103 (1958), pp. 473-478.

[28] Dorothy M. Morris, "A Study of Some of the Factors Involved in Lip-Reading" (Master's Thesis, Smith College, 1944).

scores as the length of the sentences increased. Also, a word was harder to understand when placed in a long sentence than when placed in a shorter sentence; but, the lipreadability of a sentence was not markedly influenced by its position within a group of sentences. The position of the groups of sentences did not have any noticeable effect upon lipreading performance. Taaffe and Wong[29] attempted to isolate those stimulus variables related to the ease or difficulty with which the material could be lipread. The Iowa Film Test of Lip Reading provided the stimulus materials to be analyzed. This filmed test was presented to a group of normal hearing college students, and an extensive analysis was made of the materials in terms of sentence order, sentence length, number of words in a sentence, number of syllables in a sentence, and number of vowels and consonants. Also included was an analysis of the influence of parts of speech and visibility of sounds on lipreading. It appeared that lipreading performance was affected by the number of words in a sentence, the number of syllables in a sentence, and the number of vowels and consonants, as well as the length of the stimulus words. The visibility of consonants, vowels, words, and phrases was evaluated by O'Neill.[30] He found that vision contributed 29.5% to the recognition of vowels, 57% for consonants, 38.6% for words and 17.4% for phrases. The visual recognition scores for vowels were, 76% [o], 74% [i], 68% [e], 64% [u], 63% [ʊ], 58% [ɛ], and 58% [ɪ]; and for consonants, 86% [s], 84% [f], 83% [ʃ], 80% [p], 77% [k], 75% [θ] and 71% [t]. Vision had the greatest apparent effect in the identification of consonants, and lesser effects, in order, on the recognition of vowels, words and phrases. Sumby and Pollack[31] investigated the contributions of visual factors to oral speech intelligibility as a function of the speech-to-noise ratio and the size of the possible vocabulary. They found that the visual contribution to speech intelligibility increased as the speech-to-noise ratio was decreased (less intense speech signal). This visual contribution also occurred with an increase in vocabulary size (8 words to 256 words). In a somewhat similar study, Neely[32] found that the addition of visual cues to

[29] Gordon Taaffe and Wilson Wong, "Studies of Variables in Lip Reading Stimulus Material," *John Tracy Clinic Research Papers*, III (December 1957).

[30] John J. O'Neill, "Contributions of the Visual Components of Oral Symbols to Speech Comprehension," *Journal of Speech and Hearing Disorders*, 19 (1954), pp. 429-439.

[31] W. H. Sumby and I. Pollack, "Visual Contribution to Speech Intelligibility in Noise," *Journal of the Acoustical Society of America*, 26 (1954), pp. 212-215.

[32] Keith K. Neely, "Effect of Visual Factors on the Intelligibility of Speech," *Journal of the Acoustical Society of America*, 28 (1956), pp. 1275-1277.

auditory cues raised the intelligibility of received speech some twenty per cent. Also, the distance of a listener from the speaker did not have a significant effect on listener intelligibility scores within three- to nine-foot limits.

Reams,[33] in a study investigating the relationship between the experiences of identifying words through visual sensory stimulation and auditory stimulation, found that the obtained correlation coefficients were not sufficiently high enough to indicate any positive relationship between auditory intelligibility and visual identification of the same stimulus materials. Normal hearing college students served as experimental subjects. They viewed a specially prepared silent motion picture film which utilized the Waco multiple-choice intelligibility tests. The same subjects also listened to tape recordings of the same stimulus materials spoken by the speakers who appeared on the filmed test. Woodward [34] attempted to apply the principles of structural linguistics to the study of lipreading stimulus materials. Three categories of analysis were proposed—phonological, grammatical and lexical. Sets of stimuli consisting of syllable pairs (consonant-vowel combinations) were filmed while spoken by one female speaker. The basic hypothesis under consideration was that absolute visibility of phonation was a function of the area of articulation. Normal hearing subjects merely judged whether the stimulus pairs were the same or different. In light of the data collected, the following sets of initial English consonants were classified in homophonous clusters:

$$p - b - m$$
$$f - v$$
$$wh - w - r$$
$$\overline{}$$
$$ch - dz - sh - zh - y$$
$$t - d - n - l - s - z - \theta - \text{d}$$
$$k - g - h$$

Furthermore, it was stated that if lipreaders were to distinguish among the members of these sets, it must be on the basis of phonetic, lexical, or grammatical redundancy, for the articulatory differences among them are not noticeable in visual observation.

[33] Mary H. Reams, "An Experimental Study Comparing the Visual Accompaniments of Word Identification and the Auditory Experience of Word Intelligibility" (Masters Thesis, Ohio State University Department of Speech, 1950).
[34] Mary F. Woodward, "Linguistic Methodology in Lip Reading Research," *John Tracy Clinic Research Papers*, IV (December 1957).

Brannon and Kodman[35] investigated the variables that contributed to the visual identification of monosyllabic words. Comparisons were made in terms of skilled and unskilled lipreaders. These two groups did not differ in their ability to lipread isolated words. However, in terms of scores obtained on the Utley Sentence test, which had been presented in a face to face situation, the skilled lipreaders were superior to the unskilled ones. The visibility of the total movement form afforded the best cue for visual identification of a word. Differences in the size of the vertical mouth opening, the familiarity of the word, and the phonetic length of the one-syllable words did not play significant roles in the correct identification of words. The authors also reported that the visual identification of words was directly related to the place of articulation. Thus, the lip sounds were most visible, while the sounds made in the back of the mouth were least visible.

The analysis of the stimulus materials used in lipreading is a very profitable research area. In fact, this area seems to offer the greatest possibility for future, controlled research.

The Speaker or Sender

Pauls[36] preferred the use of the term *speech reading* in preference to *lipreading*. She stated that we watch not only the movements of the speaker's lips, but also his gestures and the expression of his face. On the other hand, Mason[37] preferred the term *visual hearing* for the speech movements discernible on a speaker's face involve not merely the mobility of the lips, but also the rapid interplay of facial muscles marking the emotional lights and shadows which betray the speaker's thought.

As part of a larger study, O'Neill [38] investigated the significant differences among three speakers in terms of their ability to convey information visually or auditorily. He found that the speaker who conveyed the most information by visual means (lipreading) was also the most intelligible under nonvisual conditions.

[35] John B. Brannon, Jr., and Frank Kodman, Jr., "The Perceptual Process in Speech Reading," *A.M.A. Archives of Otolaryngology,* 70 (1959), pp. 114-119.
[36] M. D. Pauls, "Speech Reading," *Hearing and Deafness,* ed. H. Davis (Murray Hill Books, New York, 1947), Chapter 9.
[37] Marie K. Mason, "Visual Hearing: A Motion Picture Method of Instruction," *Auditory Outlook* (1932).
[38] John J. O'Neill, "Contributions of the Visual Components of Oral Symbols to the Speech Comprehension of Listeners With Normal Hearing" (Doctoral dissertation, Ohio State University Department of Speech, 1951).

An extensive study of the effects of speaker characteristics upon lipreading was done by Stone.[39] He evaluated the influences of three variables of facial context upon lipreading. The three variables under study included facial exposure, facial expression and lip mobility. Colored motion pictures of a trained actor were presented to 256 normal hearing college students. Test results indicated that better lipreading performance occurred when the speaker utilized a normal lip movement as opposed to a tight lip movement. Secondly, when the speaker's expression was plainly set rather than smiling, he was lipread with greater success. Degree of facial exposure was significant only when considered along with lip mobility and facial expression. The author also pointed out that full torso exposure was usually preferable to a limited mouth exposure. Byers and Lieberman[40] evaluated the effects of various rates of speaker presentation of materials. Silent motion picture films of a female speaker were presented to good and poor lipreaders from a residential school for the deaf. Changes in speaker rate were produced by variations in the speed of filming and projection. Thus it was possible to study four speaking rates. The results of the study indicated that the slowing down of a speaker's rate had no significant effect upon lipreading performance.

This chapter has surveyed the bulk of published material relating to research in lipreading. To be sure, much of the unpublished graduate research has been neglected. However, it is hoped that this brief review will lead to the uncovering of additional research material; and also that the framework suggested may be conducive to further research in terms of a definite, organized approach.

Few statements can be offered about the attributes of a good lipreader or the effects of environment upon lipreading; however, the nature of the lipreading stimulus and the characteristics of the speaker or sender do have some effect upon lipreading; and in short, there are many interesting possibilities open for research in the area of lipreading.

Glossary

1. *Case-Ruch Test of Spatial Relations:* paper and pencil test; 32 designs that can be completed by assembling the proper parts; measures the ability to perceive rapidly and accurately relationships among objects in space.

[39] Louis Stone, "Facial Cues of Context in Lip Reading," *John Tracy Clinic Research Papers,* V (December 1957).
[40] V. W. Byers and L. Lieberman, "Lipreading Performance and the Rate of the Speaker," *Journal of Speech and Hearing Research,* 2 (1959), pp. 271-276.

2. *Delayed auditory feedback:* the delaying, by electomechanical means, of the person's hearing of his own speech.
3. *Fragmentary sentences:* employed by Simmons* in the study of the synthetic ability of lipreaders; consisted of parts of 100 sentences requiring completion.
4. *Hanfmann-Kasanin Test:* consists of 22 blocks of five different colors and four different shapes; the subject is required to sort the blocks into four categories; the test essentially samples concept formation (nonverbal) in terms of a problem solving setting.
5. *Knower-Dusenbury Test of Ability to Judge Emotions:* paper and pencil test; photographs of male and female during speech and while expressing emotions; eleven items for each speaker.
6. *Knower Speech Attitude Scale:* paper and pencil test; 48 items; measures attitudes toward speech.
7. *Rotter Level of Aspiration Test:* utilizes the Rotter Level of Aspiration Board and is a motor performance type of test; the subject makes prediction as to future performance on the basis of previous performance, which provides a means of studying the effects of success and failure on the explicitly set goals of an individual.
8. *Visual memory span:* a measure of the number of items that can be correctly recalled or reproduced after controlled presentation of a visual stimulus.

* A. A. Simmons, "Factors Related to Lipreading," *Journal of Speech and Hearing Research,* 2 (1959), pp. 340-352.

5

THE EARLY LIPREADING TEXTS, ESPECIALLY THOSE WRIT-
ten by Nitchie and Bruhn, placed great emphasis upon
the value of eye training. Nitchie[1] listed three factors
that make for successful lipreading: Physical, mental,
and spiritual. Nitchie stated, "The physical factor is the
eyes. This is the obvious factor; so obvious, in fact, that
teachers sometimes forget its serious limitations."

Nitchie granted that the eye could not possibly handle all the problems encountered in lipreading—the
obscurity of many of the movements, the rapidity of
all the movements, the homophenity of many of the
sounds, and the variation of movements and of mouths.

The method of eye training suggested by Nitchie was
based on lipreading practice itself and not on the training of visual skill. Nitchie stressed the consideration of
accuracy, quickness, and visual memory. Training in

[1] Edward B. Nitchie, *Principles and Methods of Teaching Lipreading*
(New York: Nitchie School of Lip Reading, Inc., n.d.), pp. 1-13.

VISUAL TRAINING AND VISUAL METHODS

accuracy depended upon recognition of verbal items through contrast practice, and upon learning of movement patterns by repetitive observational practice. In other words, training in accuracy was dependent upon rote recall without consideration for thought units. Quickness of the eyes involved the development of accuracy under conditions of speeded up presentation and constant review work. The training of visual memory included practice in the increasing of visual memory span, that is, practice in recognizing increasing numbers of consecutively presented words.

Bruhn[2] stressed that the lipreader should be trained in the art of *noticing*. The eye must perceive, distinguish, and combine the externally visible characteristic movements of the organs of speech.

While these two methods stressed the importance of eye training, very little time was spent on a discussion of specific methods to be used. The training suggested involved only a form of motor learning; in other words the old adage, "practice makes perfect."

Very little formal attention has been paid to eye training, or in more fitting terminology, the teaching of visual awareness. In 1949, Glorig[3] stated that the personnel of the Audiology Center at Walter Reed Hospital felt that the basic requirement for good speech reading was good observation. Wooley,[4] in a companion article, discussed the use of the tachistoscope in teaching lipreading. Lipreading students were trained to recognize visual materials presented at rapid exposure rates. In the conclusion of her article, Wooley stated that "by use of the tachistoscope as a visual aid we hope to widen the student's span of vision, increase his quickness and accuracy of observation, and enlarge his 'unitary seeing'."

The development of attention span through the use of visual aids (flash cards, filmstrips and slides) was discussed by Bartlett,[5] who felt that such training should increase the student's attention span as well as his ability to observe essentials and ideas.

[2] Martha Bruhn, *The Mueller-Walle Method of Lip Reading for the Hard of Hearing* (Boston: M. H. Leavis, 1947).

[3] Aram Glorig, "Visual Aids in Speech Reading Instruction," *Hearing News*, 17 (10) (1949), p. 1 and 16.

[4] Florence T. W. Wooley, "How We Use the Tachistoscope," *Hearing News*, 17 (10) (1949), pp. 3-4.

[5] Ruth Bartlett, "Attention in Speech Reading," *Hearing News*, 17 (3) (1949), pp. 1-2, 18-22.

A Suggested Approach

Before approaching the problem of visual training, a brief description will be given of the areas of visual skill to be explored. Also, the training goals will be established. The three major goals to be considered are:

1. Practice in visual perception
2. Development of attention span
3. Development of concentration

Visual Perception

Visual perception involves training in the recognition of items in the visual world. Areas of training can be grouped under four headings—perceptual field, peripheral field, synthetic ability, and figure ground recognition. For example, if a simple visual target is used, the subject merely reproduces the pattern he sees. The subject's visual attention can be centered by having the figures or stimulus objects closely grouped in the center of the target. By increasing the number of figures, however, recognition span is increased; and by spreading out the figures, the subject develops peripheral viewing abilities. This approach is illustrated by Figures 5, 6, and 7.

To make the materials more meaningful, words instead of abstract figures can be used. Figures 8, 9, and 10 best illustrate this type of approach. Figure 8 lists four words that compose a sentence, but the words are placed in scrambled order. The subject must make a sentence from the words. Figures 9 and 10 give examples of truncated words. The subject again must develop a sentence from the display. Such an approach adds the extra dimension of semantic knowledge. This type of material can be presented via flash cards or prepared slides. Such training moves from meaningless materials (forms) to meaningful materials (words).

Training in figure ground recognition involves the recognition of an embedded figure, or the separation of a basic figure from a part of a larger *whole*. For example, in Figure 11 a simple figure is presented in a matrix of diagonal lines. Under conditions of rapid exposure, the subject's task is to recognize the basic stimulus material (the figure). In this way the viewer learns to look for the essential and disregard the background distraction.

FIGURE 5. *Visual target centered. Subject is to reproduce what he sees.*

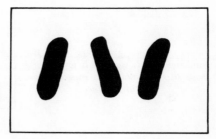

FIGURE 6. *Targets are spread out requiring the viewer to increase his viewing span.*

FIGURE 7. *Figures are spread to the extremes of the vewing area. Subject must now attend to peripheral areas.*

Attention Span

Training in this area normally involves the tachistoscope. The tachistoscope is essentially a projector with a shutter that allows for timed exposure of materials. It is possible to provide speeds of exposure from one second to 1/100th of a second. The slides used for such projection can consist of individual 2″ by 2″ slides or multiple or single 3″ by 4″ slides. A target area, usually a screen, is used for exposure of the materials. A focusing point is suggested, either a definite spot placed on the screen or commands to look at the center of the screen just before each slide is projected. Time of projection is matched to the visual ability of the subjects. The authors believe that a moderate speed, 1/25th of a second, is the best speed for initial projection. If a slower speed is used, subjects are inclined to

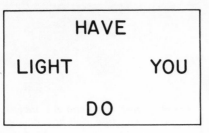

HAVE

LIGHT   YOU

DO

FIGURE 8. *Simple word groupings. Subject is to place words in such an order that they will make a meaningful sentence.*

FIGURE 9. *Word groupings with two truncated words. Subject is to organize these stimulus materials into a meaningful sentence.*

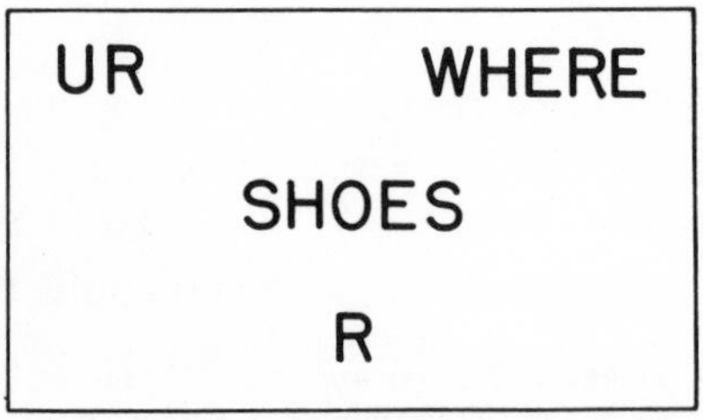

LIKE

BE-STAK

DO   U

UR   WHERE

SHOES

R

FIGURE 10. *Word groupings similar to those in Figure 9. However, there is a greater degree of truncation.*

develop faulty viewing habits, and more rapid speeds tend to discourage subjects. (However, as training proceeds, more rapid rates of projection can be introduced. It is well to devote a maximum of ten minutes per lesson to such practice.) The slides can consist of photographs of abstract shapes, words, sentences, or photographs of specific situations. In fact, it is possible to utilize materials similar to those previously described in the discussion of flash cards. Rather complete descriptions of the rationale of tachistoscopic training as well as descriptions of tachistoscopic training methods are provided by Barnette[6] and Renshaw.[7]

Another important area in such training is that of *closure*. Gestalt psychologists, who view immediate experiences as being organized

[6] G. C. Barnette, *Learning Through Seeing* (Dubuque, Iowa. William C. Brown, 1951).
[7] S. Renshaw, *Tachistoscopic Procedure* (Columbus, Ohio: mimeographed material, Ohio State University, 1945).

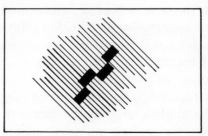

Figure 11. *Basic pattern imbedded in a matrix of diagonal lines. The viewer is to reproduce the pattern represented by the four dark squares.*

in wholes, describe closure as an ability to view items in terms of sequence patterns, or familiar patterns. Thus, closure involves perceptual grouping on the basis of past similarities and the innate organization properties of the stimulus materials. Visual training in this area, then, involves training in the ability to exclude the irrelevant and to organize materials on the basis of observed similarities. Practice begins with slides depicting a series of dots. The slides are projected at rapid rates of exposure; and the dots are arranged in discrete clusters, in patterns utilizing various colors, in directional configurations, or in such a fashion that a basic design is presented except for three to five dots that are out of place. This latter technique could be expanded by having more and more of the dots assume random positions, and an arrangement of this sort could be continued until the entire pattern is destroyed. Also, slides could be made of the test plates that appear in the Raven's Progressive Matrices[8] and the Case-Ruch Test of Spatial Relations.[9]

After practice with the viewing of figures, the subject can move on to slides containing scrambled words. Within this matrix of scrambled words, a common phrase can be developed, and the viewer must select the phrase out of the welter of words. Further levels of such training can include slides containing more words and two or three phrases. The process of placing parts into a whole is similar to the process of synthesizing mentioned in several of the lipreading texts. In other words, if the stimulus material is viewed as meaningful communication material, the isolated elements can be arranged into a meaningful unit.

Students of lipreading should be aware of the statistical probabilities of the English language. Redundancy, or repetitions, leads to a great deal of predictability—especially in the instance of lipreading.

[8] Progressive Matrices, Sets A,B,C,D and E (1938) (London: H. K. Lewis and Co., Ltd.).
[9] H. W. Case and F. Ruch, *Manual of Directions, Survey of Space Relations Ability, Form A* (Los Angeles, California Test Bureau, 1944).

In the terminology of information theory,[10] lipreading is a form of communication that yields a great deal of information since more information is gained if a correct response is made from a wide range of equally likely alternatives, as opposed to a correct response made from two alternatives.

Lipreading students can be taught to deal with predictabilities of the English language by means of sentence completion practice; or better yet, they can participate in "word guessing" games as described by Black and Moore.[11] Words were removed at random from selected sentences. In the first instance, only one word was removed from each sentence. Thereafter, two, three, four, five, six, and seven words were removed. The remaining words were retyped with no spaces left for those that had been taken out. Subjects were then told to construct probable sentences from these various word groupings.

This visual form training accomplishes two purposes for the student of lipreading, (1) the development of visual concentration and (2) the development of synthetic ability. The first accomplishment is obvious—the subject learns that he must be alert if he is to recognize the stimulus materials. The second accomplishment is a little more difficult to explain. The subject develops the basic set to view visual stimuli as wholes, and not as parts, or isolated units. If he is asked to reproduce a complicated stimulus, he will find, if he tends to catalogue individual items rather than a general impression, that he will miss most of the pertinent information. Similarly, if in lipreading practice, he is searching for individual words he will miss the entire sentence or the thought of the material.

One of the better methods for bridging the gap between visual and lipreading practice involves the use of covers from popular magazines. The subject is taken through a period of training which is directed toward the retaining of the thought of the picture, rather than the memory for small details. He must use rapid, retentive behavior in such a task. The instructor presents the magazine cover, through slide projections or by means of mounted flash cards. The student views the picture for five or ten seconds. Then the picture is removed and the subject is questioned about it. The questions can be given without voice or with very low voice. If the student cannot recall too many details, the instructor can give, via lipreading, a

[10] C. E. Shannon and W. Weaver, *The Mathematical Theory of Communication* (Urbana: University of Illinois Press, 1949).

[11] J. W. Black and W. E. Moore, *Speech: Code, Meaning and Communication* (New York: McGraw-Hill Book Co., 1955), p. 96.

short description of the picture. Then questions can be asked a second time. After this initial approach, questions can be directed toward specifics, that is, how many people are there in the picture, or what are some of the objects in the background? Thus, the subject is directed toward an approach that treats the viewing of the whole as an entirely different experience from the viewing of parts separately. A modification of this pattern involves the use of cartoons found in magazines and newspapers. All captions and conversational representations are removed. The student is then asked, after a short exposure of the cartoon, what a good title for the picture would be, or what the people are saying. Another modification is to provide the students with the captions or the conversation beforehand, then match them to the appropriate cartoon. In this way, the subject looks for thoughts—as he should in a lipreading situation.

One other method includes the production of slides or filmstrips of individual lip movements for the various phonetic elements. These representations are presented at various speeds of exposure until the subjects have learned to recognize all of the movements. The next step combines individual phonetic patterns into words. For example, the lip movements for the consonants [k] and [t] and the vowel [æ] can be placed together for the word cat. With sufficient speeds of projection, the elisions occurring in everyday speech can be reproduced. This method is used with near point as well as far point tachistoscopic presentation. Photographs of lip movements associated with the major consonants and vowels of the English language are presented in Figure 12, pp. 59-67.

Concentration

Visual concentration is improved by utilizing the techniques described above, but with rapid rates of projection. Thus, by stepping up the rate of presentation, the subject is required to develop increased ability to concentrate.

Another method used in the development of concentration is situational practice or skits, or even charades. To be able to decipher pantomime is immensely valuable. Thus, if the subject is familiar with the symbolic aspects of nonverbal communication, he can use these cues, along with the verbal cues (lip movements), to supplement his communication patterns. In this respect, it is necessary for the lipreading therapist to read the materials presented by Efron[12]

[12] David Efron, *Gesture and Environment* (New York: King's Crown Press, 1941).

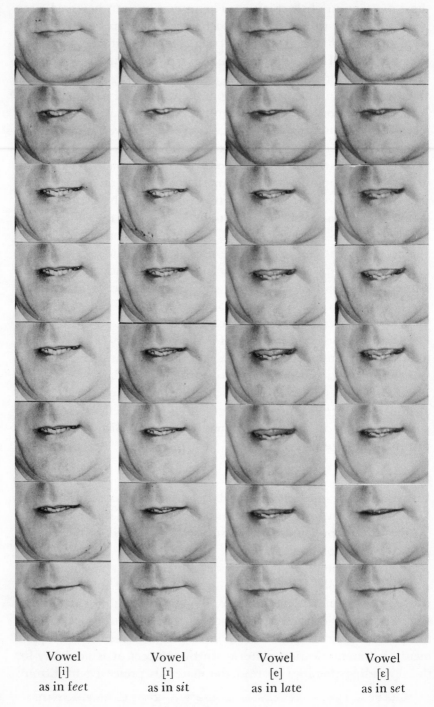

Vowel	Vowel	Vowel	Vowel
[i]	[ɪ]	[e]	[ɛ]
as in f*ee*t	as in s*i*t	as in l*a*te	as in s*e*t

FIGURE 12. *Mouth postures involved in the production of selected vowels and consonants.*

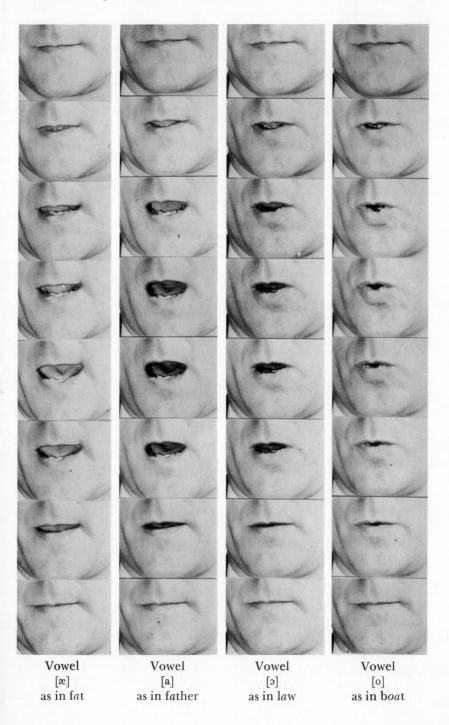

Vowel	Vowel	Vowel	Vowel
[æ]	[a]	[ɔ]	[o]
as in fat	as in father	as in law	as in boat

(Continued)

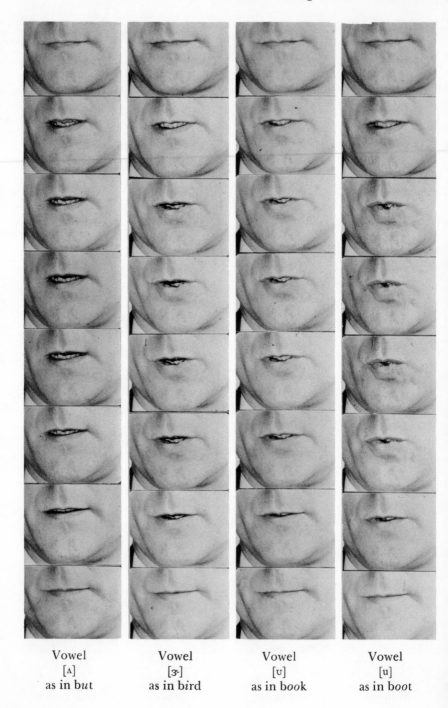

| Vowel
[ʌ]
as in b*u*t | Vowel
[ɝ]
as in b*i*rd | Vowel
[ʊ]
as in b*oo*k | Vowel
[u]
as in b*oo*t |

(Continued)

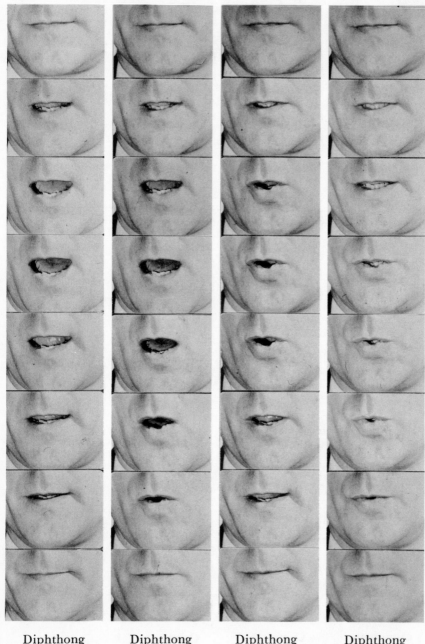

Diphthong [aɪ] as in b*i*te

Diphthong [aʊ] as in gr*ou*nd

Diphthong [ɔɪ] as in b*oy*

Diphthong [ɪu] as in f*ew*

(Continued)

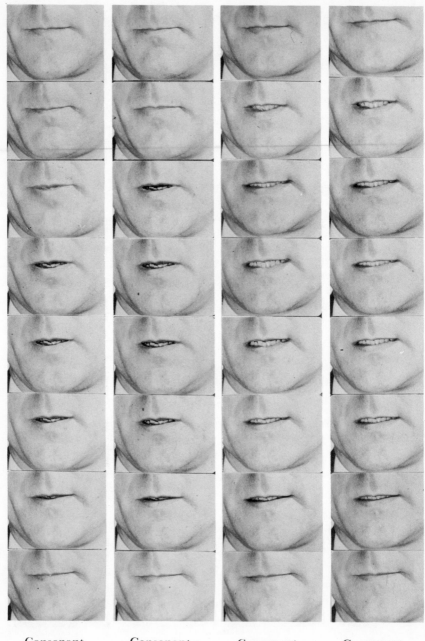

Consonant	Consonant	Consonant	Consonant
[p]	[b]	[t]	[d]
as in *p*ay	as in *b*y	as in *t*o	as in *d*ay

(Continued)

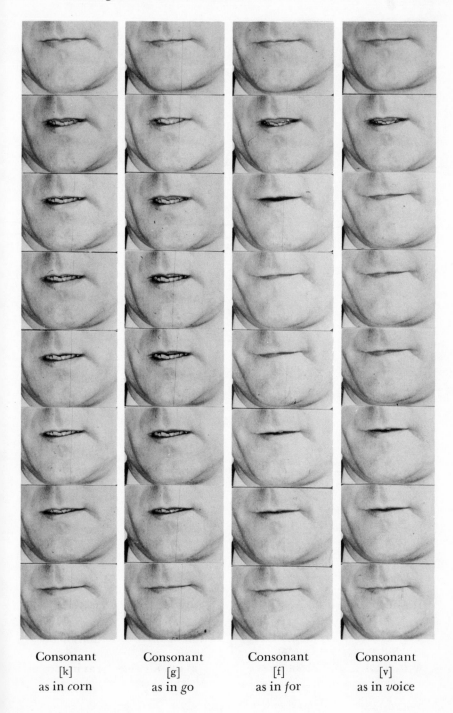

Consonant [k] as in *c*orn

Consonant [g] as in *g*o

Consonant [f] as in *f*or

Consonant [v] as in *v*oice

(Continued)

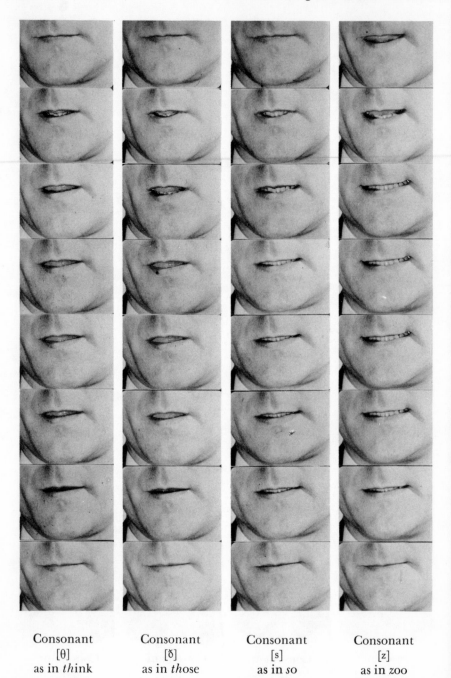

Consonant [θ] as in *th*ink

Consonant [ð] as in *th*ose

Consonant [s] as in *s*o

Consonant [z] as in *z*oo

(Continued)

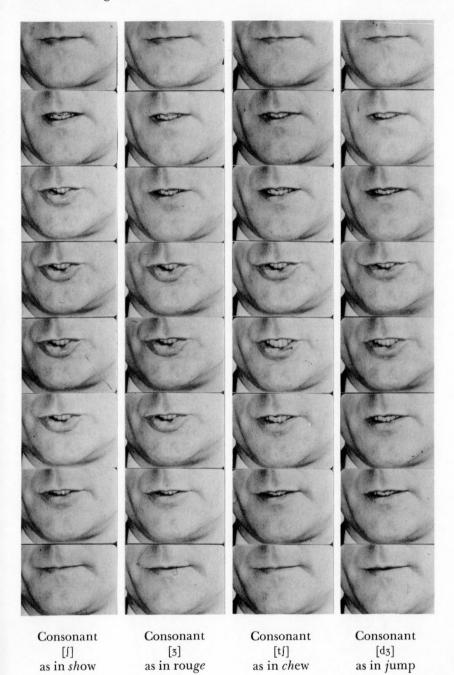

| Consonant
[ʃ]
as in *sh*ow | Consonant
[ʒ]
as in rou*ge* | Consonant
[tʃ]
as in *ch*ew | Consonant
[dʒ]
as in *j*ump |

(Continued)

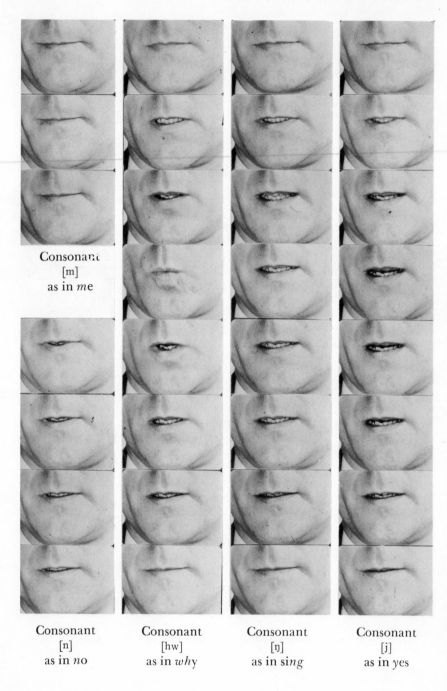

Consonant
[m]
as in *m*e

Consonant   Consonant   Consonant   Consonant
[n]   [hw]   [ŋ]   [j]
as in *n*o   as in *wh*y   as in si*ng*   as in *y*es

(Continued)

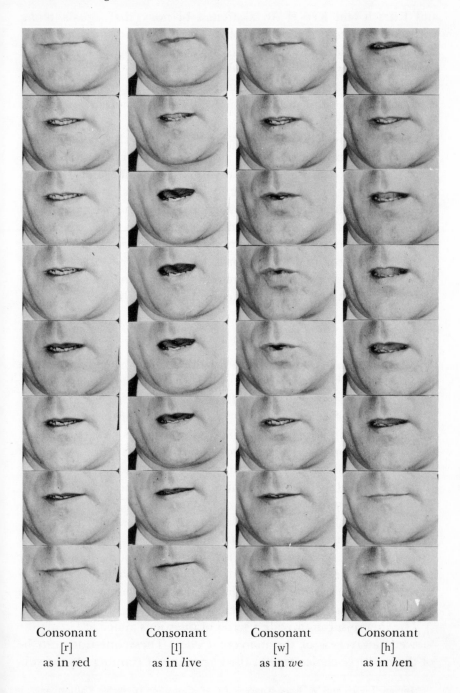

| Consonant
[r]
as in *r*ed | Consonant
[l]
as in *l*ive | Consonant
[w]
as in *w*e | Consonant
[h]
as in *h*en |

and Ruesch and Kees.[13] An awareness of nonverbal signals, along with even a partial recognition of the verbal symbols, will help improve communication. Thus, skits with their changing direction of the flow of communication, charades with their pantomimic practice, and situational skits with their utilization of props and connected discourse, will help the lipreader develop a concentration that should become habitual.

The authors have found a dual carry-over from classroom practice to daily, communication practice. This dual carry-over is pronounced with some individuals, while with others, only one aspect occurs. The first of these carry-over patterns involves visual awareness. The individual is more alert to all visual stimuli. The second form is the most important. In this instance, the subject is ready to view all visual stimuli as meaningful communication materials. Everything that is said or gestured makes sense. Many times the interjection of visual training stops a subject from word searching. He is given a new orientation to lipreading—he is doing visual listening!

Motion Pictures

Additional visual training can be provided through the use of silent motion picture films especially produced for training in lipreading. There are two such series—the Mason Visual Hearing Series and the Morkovin Life Situation Motion Picture Series. Of these two series, the Morkovin films offer the greatest opportunity for visual practice. It is possible for the viewer of these films to react to the nonverbal aspects of the lipreading situations, depicted in them. In this series there are ten films showing situations, such as The Family Dinner, At The Grocery Store, and so forth. If the viewer is to fully understand what is occurring in the film, he must be aware of the nature of each situation, of the individuals in the film, of the gestures they use, and of the background. By rerunning such films, it is possible to develop increased visual attention. Thus, the would-be lipreader must not only read the lips of the speakers, but he must recall the visual details that accompany each situation.

The therapist can provide a series of questions aimed at testing the viewer's awareness of the nonverbal cues. These questions can be of the multiple-choice type at the beginning of training. As the sub-

[13] Jurgen Ruesch and W. Kees, *Nonverbal Communication* (Berkeley, California: University of California Press, 1956).

ject becomes more proficient, he can be asked to write down answers to the questions. The questions can be so structured that they can check observations of characters, actions, backgrounds, and so on. In this way he can develop visual attention as well as an improved visual awareness.

Some visual props are used in the Mason films. These may include a picture, an object, a gesture, or a glance. If the subject is ready to utilize these cues, they will aid him in lipreading the materials being presented. Also, questions can be directed toward the subject's observation of the physical characteristics of the speaker, such as the color of his eyes, hair, or clothes. Since the films are in technicolor, they expand the subject's viewing field to still another area, that of color.

It is felt that the viewing of regular motion pictures can be of little value because the situations are not as well structured as in the films especially prepared for lipreading. It is better not to include such films in a visual training program.

One final area related to visual training is television viewing. Many therapists tell their lipreading students to watch television for lipreading practice. However, only certain types of television programs afford opportunities for lipreading and visual training. Programs utilizing pantomime, or full face shots, and quiz shows utilizing visual score boards offer the best opportunity for visual practice. A more complete discussion of the use of television in lipreading instruction occurs in Chapter 11.

The suggestions made in this chapter should serve as mere starting points. The ingenuity of trained therapists will motivate them to make use of many more aspects of visual training. In fact, the relationship of visual skill to lipreading ability is one of the frontier areas for research. The eye should be brought back into the lipreading picture!

6

THE COMBINED USE OF VISUAL AND AUDITORY MODALITIES in aural rehabilitation seems to be an established, if not necessary approach. However, many therapists stress only one form of rehabilitative procedure. A great deal of verbal emphasis is placed upon a combined approach, but in actual practice, major attention is directed toward the use of only one of the sensory modalities. Auditory training is neglected, with the result that lipreading becomes the major therapeutic technique. The existence of residual hearing is accepted but very little auditory training is provided. Such an approach is especially prominent in the majority of the public school programs. Auditory training, when it does occur, is confined to the audiology clinic. Even in this instance, it receives only moderate attention. In some cases, lack of interest may be attributed to the reluctance to manipulate equipment or to the lack of equipment and appropriate materials, in other instances, lack of experience

LIPREADING, AUDITORY TRAINING AND HEARING AIDS

in auditory training contributes to its neglect. The therapist must remember that all hard of hearing persons have some residual hearing. Aural rehabilitation work should be directed toward the use of this residual hearing and not toward the determination of how well the individual can do without it. Lipreading has value for the hard of hearing as a supplementary or additive communication channel.

In this chapter, methods of blending lipreading instruction with auditory training will be discussed. In essence, stress will be placed upon the fact that lipreading is not independent of auditory reception. Most of the published manuals dealing with auditory training emphasize materials and techniques. Except in rare instances, very little effort has been made to present suggestions for the use of lipreading along with the auditory training. The suggestions that follow will be confined to a discussion of how lipreading can be coordinated with auditory training. Major attention is directed toward lipreading, under the assumption that the reader will be familiar with the conventional approaches to auditory training.

Areas to Be Considered in Combined Practice

The vital factor in any aural rehabilitation program is the degree of improvement that occurs because of such a program. To determine this, tests must be administered at the beginning of a therapy program, during the program, and at the termination of therapy. In this way, areas of difficulty can be ascertained and the results of therapy can be evaluated in terms of improvement for visual and auditory performance. A measure of improvement should be obtained in lipreading alone, and auditory reception alone, as well as when both sensory channels are being used. Special tests that evaluated the effects of the various channels working alone and in combination were developed at the Clarke School for the Deaf by Quick[1] and Hudgins and Numbers.[2] These tests have been labeled *listen, look* and *listen and look* tests. Johnson[3] originated a series of tests which were called tests of *acoustic understanding, speech reading* and *speech reading* and *acoustic understanding.* Results indicated that

[1] Marian Quick, "A Speech Perception Test to Measure the Achievement of Young Children in Acoustic Training" (Master's Thesis, Smith College, 1949).

[2] C. V. Hudgins and Mary E. Numbers, "Speech Perception in Present Day Education for Deaf Children," *The Volta Review,* 50 (1948), pp. 449-456.

[3] Elizabeth H. Johnson, "Testing Results of Acoustic Training," *American Annals of the Deaf,* 84 (1939), pp. 223-233.

speech perception scores increased as hearing supplemented vision. However, if such comparisons are to be made, the voice level of the speaker must remain constant from one testing condition to another. (A meter to monitor speech output can be employed.) Only then can definite statements be made regarding the level of improvement and the value of vision plus audition. Hutton, Curry, and Armstrong[4] have developed a set of testing materials to be used in the evaluation of auditory, visual, and combined auditory-visual discrimination ability, as well as to indicate the particular phonema that are difficult for the subject to recognize. The authors reported that a combined score (visual—auditory) gave a better indication of the benefit the subject gained from visual clues than did the visual score alone.

The above article has additional relevance, for attention was focused on the types of stimulus materials that are difficult for the hard of hearing individual and stress was placed upon their use in training. Another report on these testing materials was presented by Hutton[5] who said that combined auditory and visual clues resulted in greater intelligibility than either audition or vision alone. Also, in most instances, visual stimuli alone did not provide sufficient clues for adequate communication.

Equipment

If combined training is to be undertaken, proper equipment is required. The basic pieces of equipment should include a sound source (microphone, turntable or tape deck), amplifiers with a flat type of response, attenuators to provide adequate control of the basic speech and noise signals, filters to approximate various types of listening spectra, monitoring meters (VU meters) to insure adequate control of all inputs, and quality earphones and loudspeakers. Bangs and Shapley[6] have provided an excellent discussion of the type of equipment to be used in the auditory training of young children. The unit they describe is one that can be used with children and adults with severe aural handicaps.

In all probability, auditory training is in its present state because few of the commercial auditory training units allow for convenient

[4] Charles Hutton, E. T. Curry, and M. B. Armstrong, "Semidiagnostic Test Materials for Aural Rehabilitation," *Journal of Speech and Hearing Disorders,* 24 (1959), pp. 319-329.

[5] Charles Hutton, "Combining Auditory and Visual Stimuli," *The Volta Review,* 61 (1959), pp. 316-319.

[6] Tina E. Bangs and James L. Shapley, "Group Auditory Training Unit for Preschool Children," *Journal of Speech and Hearing Disorders,* 18 (1953), pp. 366-372.

reference levels. In other words, they are not calibrated to a base level of .0002 dynes/cm², but rather they utilize such meaningless terms as 120 db, 130 db or plus 30, or simple lined increments. Thus the therapist can rarely match stimulus input to the degree and type of hearing loss. At the present time, levels are either set by a chance system or a monitoring system where the subject is asked if the tone is loud enough or soft enough. Also, when a microphone is used without a monitoring device, therapists have no idea of their own voice level. Thus, it is not possible to develop any objective evaluation of starting points or degrees of improvement.

Another area to be considered is that of the development of auditory tolerance. If auditory tolerance (ability to withstand high levels of sound) increases, the auditory area will be enlarged. Not only will the individual be able to withstand higher levels of amplification, he will also experience an increase in the number of auditory cues he can use. Again, if a realistic measure of improvement of auditory tolerance is to be made, it will be necessary to have an objective scale. Thus the therapist must speak in terms of intensity levels.

If such equipment is not available and the patient's hearing loss is slight, the therapist can give auditory training in orthotelephonic fashion (free field without amplification). However, it is still imperative that the therapist maintain a constant voice level and give careful consideration to the selection of testing and training materials. An approach which does not use amplified sound in such training was described by Browd [7] who provided a list of training materials and techniques. A set of exercises utilizing alphabet letters and monosyllabic words without amplification was developed by Kelly [8] who suggested that the best measure of the student's ability in face to face conversation occurred when speech was heard and seen.

Materials

Many of the basic approaches used in auditory training stress the recognition of individual sounds. Such an approach operates on the assumption that learning should progress from individual units to larger units or wholes. Stimulus materials are selected in terms of specific sounds (nonsense syllables, individual sounds or mono-

[7] Victor L. Browd, *The New Way to Better Hearing* (New York: Crown Publishers, 1951).

[8] J. C. Kelly, *Audio-Visual Speech Reading* (Mimeographed manual, Urbana: University of Illinois Department of Speech, 1955).

syllabic words), or complex sounds (polysyllabic words or short phrases), or connected discourse (sentences, paragraphs and stories). Monosyllabic words can be obtained from the original Harvard word lists[9] or from a prepared listing of monosyllabic words.[10] In this latter listing the words are arranged according to sounds. A three component plan has been followed. Items with the same vowel sound are in a single column, with a listing of the beginning sound as well as the ending sound for each of the combinations. Thus a pool of some 9000 monosyllabic words grouped according to phonetic similarities are available for use. The polysyllabic words and phrases can be obtained from several sources. The equated phrases developed by Walker and Black[11] are excellent materials since they are equated for length and intensity. For studies in connected discourse, excellent sources are the practices and test materials used by those working in the field of *listening*. Other sources of materials are listed at the end of the chapter.

Test and practice materials for consonants should also be mentioned. Specific consonant materials known as the Larsen Consonant Discrimination Test are available on discs. The Larsen album contains three records with two of the records serving as practice records, the third as a test record. The basic format of the records is that of a two-choice discrimination test. These materials were developed at Deshon General Hospital during the World War II period in an attempt to develop a scale for measuring the relative importance of the basic phonetic sounds in respect to frequency of occurrence and their visibility. Larsen[12] has offered suggestions on how the record can be integrated with lipreading practice. The various sounds of the English language have been arranged in terms of the order of visual difficulty of the various consonants.

Suggested Approach Utilizing Lipreading and Hearing

In spite of the theory of combined practice in training, the initial stages of aural rehabilitation give training without voice so that the

[9] James P. Egan, "Articulation Testing Methods," *Laryngoscope*, 58 (1948), pp. 955-991.

[10] H. M. Moser, J. J. Dreher, and H. J. Oyer, "One Syllable Words," *AFCRC TN* 55-56 (June 1957).

[11] Crayton Walker, and J. W. Black, "The Intrinsic Intensity of Oral Phrases," Report NM 001 064.01.02, U.S. Naval School of Aviation Medicine (May 1950).

[12] Laila Larsen, *Consonant Sound Discrimination* (University of Indiana, Bloomington, Indiana, 1950).

hard-of-hearing person can focus his attention upon the visual aspects of speech. If such an approach is not employed from the beginning, the auditory channel will be used exclusively and the subject will not try to make use of the visual cues. Only because of this initial "sensory" isolation will the individual be alerted to the use of lip-reading alone. Once he is aware of the visual channel, training can then move toward the utilization of the combined auditory-visual modalities.

It is best to start such combined practice in environmental noise situations; in other words, not in an ideal communication environment, but in one that requires concentration for both sets of modalities as well as a combination of the two. The instructor can simulate environmental noise situations by using sound effects records as backgrounds. These records can be obtained from several sources which are listed at the end of this chapter. These records simulate restaurant sounds and sounds associated with bowling alleys, railroad trains, automobiles and various sport events. This listening-in-noise training is realistic because the instructor uses voice and the practice itself takes place in a familiar situation against ordinary noise backgrounds; and this is desirable because the subject must combine audition and vision to gain meaning.

Two additional factors to consider are the level of noise and the speech-to-noise ratio. The level of noise and speech can be controlled by means of attenuators. Thus, if the outputs of the earphones and loudspeakers have been determined, it is possible to calibrate attentuator readings to sound pressure readings at the outputs of either of these two systems. Then it is possible to "read" levels of noise and speech from the attenuator readings. The ratio is the result of the settings of the attenuators for noise and for speech. A zero speech-to-noise ratio is always a good starting point, for subjects are able to hear a part of the signal but usually it is difficult listening. As the subject improves in his listening ability, the level of noise can be increased; or listening is made more difficult. In essence, as the level of noise increases, the individual must make more use of the visual channel. This type of training can only be undertaken with proper equipment. It may be divided into segments so that the major part of the lesson for the first few sessions is devoted to straight visual observation.

Charades and pantomime can be included as part of the visual training, which would not be centered around isolated sounds, but around words keyed to specific sounds. The order of progression may move from words utilizing lip sounds to words with open articulator (vowel) sounds. Part of the lesson can be devoted to the auditory discrimination of isolated sounds. Amplified sound is introduced at a subliminal or, just at threshold, level so that the individual must use minimal auditory cues along with the visual cues of lipreading. The level of amplification is slowly raised. so that the amalgamation of cues continues in a logical fashion, with initial stress on the visual aspects of communication, and a gradual transition to incorporation of auditory cues. After several weeks of such training, the lesson materials can be blended so that the same ones are used for both visual and auditory training. Thus, the student can begin to associate between visible movement and auditory discrimination. In this way, he is working toward visual listening. The practice makes him automatically aware of what is said without realizing if he is hearing or seeing it. Also, with the utilization of both his auditory and visual channels, he may be trained in the area of extra messages, that is, emotional content of speech. If he is trained to associate gestures and facial expressions with quality and rate of speech, he will be able to add to his communication efficiency. If a "phonetic" approach is used it is best to start with monosyllabic words, gradually worked into phrases and sentences. Stories can then be introduced along with visual props and lead-in sentences or printed cues. Such presentation should be of the face-to-face type.

Story retention is checked initially by means of multiple-choice answer sheets. The client checks off from a list of alternatives what he considers to be the correct answers to questions about the story he has just been given. All requested recall should be in terms of thought units rather than individual words or sentences. Some students will balk at the idea of using auditory cues. They will claim that they will not be learning how to lipread because they can hear most of the practice material. It is necessary for the therapist to point out that sound plus lipreading is the logical approach to communication.

The amplified sound can be presented in a sound field with a loud-speaker or earphones. The first method may be more realistic, but many hard of hearing people require an initial focusing of sound at the ear. Many need to relearn the meaning of various sounds including the phonetic patterns of speech.

Commercial filters can be used to shape the characteristics of the stimulus. In this way, it is possible to present materials with a low frequency, high frequency, or selected band emphasis; and guided listening practice for various types of distorted stimuli can be offered. Wedenburg[13] has suggested modification of the stimulus so that the hard of hearing person receives emphasis in the frequency range that has been most affected by the hearing loss. In other words, it is *mirror* amplification. Filtering can also provide "restricted" auditory cues to be worked in with the visual ones. Because he will be listening to distorted cues much of the time, even with amplification such practice will teach him to translate his customary distorted pattern into a meaningful one. Thus, through auditory discrimination practice and association of visual cues with auditory pattern, the person can learn to associate a distorted pattern of auditory cues with a meaningful set of visual signals. The type of training discussed above, however, is of a cortical type. The person is not going to experience any sort of peripheral improvement, but he can learn the meaning of auditory and visual cues.

The Use of Hearing Aids

The training described has not been concerned with individuals wearing hearing aids. With the wearing of an aid, however, the therapy program changes. It is necessary to substitute manipulation of the controls of an auditory training unit for the manipulation of the controls of the hearing aid. In the former case, this manipulation is undertaken by the therapist, while in the latter instance, the hard-of-hearing person does the manipulation. Thus, when the client sets the controls on his aid, it is not possible to have control over the level of the acoustic stimulus. The output of the aid should be known, especially the incremental changes that occur with the movement of the volume control. In an ideal clinical situation, a hearing aid evaluation unit can be used to determine the changes. However, most clinical settings will not be so equipped. Therefore, it is necessary to use relative levels in setting the intensity. Since many of the newer types of aids do not have volume controls that operate in discrete steps, even this may be difficult to do. As a result, adjustment of intensity levels cannot be as definite as with auditory

[13] E. Wedenburg, "Auditory Training of Deaf and Hearing Children," *Acta Oto-Laryngolgica*, 94 (1951), pp. 1-129.

training units or with hearing aids that have discrete volume steps engraved on the volume control dial.

Loudspeakers can present the stimuli with the same control as exercised with earphone listening. Similar training and testing materials can be utilized. The basic approach outlined above may also be used. However, training must be geared to the nature of the output of the hearing aid. Thus, much of the training will center around guided listening and viewing. DiCarlo[14] listed the goals of auditory training with the hearing aid as the restoration of efficient synthesis of hearing memory, anticipation of the requirements of the situation, development of visual skills, adjustment to the acquisition of meaning from reduced cues, and an increase in the knowledge of probable situational behavior. Thus therapy with an individual wearing a properly fitted hearing aid should proceed rapidly. However, there is the danger of neglecting the value of lipreading in this situation. Both the auditory and visual channels of communication must be stressed with this individual as with the non-aid wearer.

The type of approach suggested in this chapter must be adjusted to the particular needs of the individual. In Chapter 9, this individualized approach is discussed in relation to specific types of hearing problems. As will be noted in a discussion of the various case histories, auditory training and lipreading are utilized in a combined fashion.

Outline of First Four Weeks of an Aural Rehabilitation Program

To give the reader an idea of a specific rehabilitation program geared to the individual, the following description of four weeks of a program is presented. This particular program, consisting of daily half-hour sessions, was arranged for a 35 year old hard-of-hearing veteran. He exhibited an average loss of 41 decibels for the right ear and 42 decibels for the left ear. In spite of a hearing aid which had been fitted in the left ear, the subject was withdrawn from a hearing environment, for he showed a lack of alertness for either auditory or visual cues. A combined auditory training-lipreading program of rehabilitation was planned. The major aim of the program was to provide the subject with experience in the use of visual and auditory cues to supplement the use of a hearing aid. The therapy

[14] Louis M. DiCarlo, "Auditory Training for the Adult," *The Volta Review*, 50 (1948), pp. 490-494.

sessions involved one therapist; when skits were presented, an additional therapist assisted. The subject was seated approximately six feet from the therapist who either sat across a table from him, stood, or moved about the room. A conventional type classroom was used, with four loudspeakers mounted in the corners of the room. An auditory training unit with playback equipment which fed the loudspeakers, individually and in series, was a permanent installation, and a blackboard and mounting surfaces for visual aids were located on two walls. Banks of fluorescent light tubes provided an even distribution of light throughout the room.

First day:
Explanation of purpose of program. Discussion of the value of combined practice. Demonstration of contributions of vision alone, audition alone, and vision and audition together. Basic personal questions served as the stimulus materials. Administration of test of *look, listen,* and *look-listen.* Also, administration of Mason test film.

Second day:
Fifteen minutes of practice on "speech without auditory cues," followed by fifteen minutes of practice on "speech without visual cues." Discrimination materials consisted of monosyllabic words used in pairs of contrasting sounds, and in terms of phonetic composition (initial consonants of plosive character).

Third day:
Initial listening in noise practice. Sound effects records (traffic background, factory noise, and New Year's Eve background) were used to provide noise background. The noise was not set at too high a level. Practice materials included monosyllabic words from lists 7, 8, 9, and 10 of original Harvard word lists.

Fourth and fifth days:
Thirty minutes of practice of understanding individual words against interfering noises (30 minute transcriptions of radio programs involving constant speaking; informational talks, panel discussions, and "soap operas"). Individual monosyllabic words in contrasting pairs were used in the practice. Also, practice with consonants in fricative and labio-dental groupings.

Sixth and seventh days:
Practice in listening without auditory cues. Paired words differing only in vowel composition. Fifteen minutes of practice with vowel discrimination against a noise background (recordings of various environmental noises).

Eighth and ninth days:
Review of practice with selected consonants and vowels as incorporated in monosyllabic words. Used paired words with vision alone, (no voice), auditory alone (no viewing), in noise with a zero speech-to-

noise ratio, conversational practice in quiet and combined approach (vision and audition) with above materials.

Tenth day:

Discussion of hearing aids and how they assist in lipreading. Discussion of benefits of hearing aids and effects of auditory "sets," and discussion of critical listening and viewing. Practice work with aid in place, with therapist switching from voice to no voice throughout the practice period.

Eleventh day:

Practice in speech discrimination. Sentences and phrases. Viewing alone, auditory alone and combined. Listening against noise backgrounds using phrases.

Twelfth and thirteenth days:

Intelligibility practice with sentences, without voice, with voice, in noise, and in quiet. Sentence materials included paired sentences, and exercises required subject to indicate differences between two sentences, to select correct words out of a multiple-choice listing, and distinguish incorrect words that had been placed in sentences.

Fourteenth and fifteenth days:

Practice in rapid response to sentences. Series of Harvard sentences, anecdotes, and quiz questions presented in noise and quiet. Also, practice with similar materials with aid off and aid on. Rapid response in terms of thought units rather than word recognition.

Sixteenth day:

Demonstrated "whole" approach with magazine covers. Stressed recall of thoughts. Presented description of pictures with no voice, low voice, and conversational voice. Stressed need to watch carefully. Informed client that he should develop habit of indicating when he does not hear. Stressed that the hard of hearing individual must structure communication situation to his liking.

Seventeenth day:

Worked on developing tolerance for noise. Discussed fact that noise has semantic as well as acoustic aspects. Practiced listening against competing voices that were reading slightly different materials. Checked to see if subject was able to answer questions about primary materials presented by the therapist.

Eighteenth day:

Practice on colloquial forms using following subject areas: newspapers, automobiles, magazines, and cigarettes. Used intermittent noise backgrounds with combined approach. Presented skit dealing with purchasing of tickets for a play.

Nineteenth day:

Situation practice. Discussed people and objects in the clinic. Went over daily newspaper items, short stories from *Reader's Digest* and *Saturday Evening Post*. Used white noise as background. Therapist switched from voice to no voice to see how well client reacted.

Twentieth day:
Start incorporating tachistoscopic practice with five and six digit numbers presented at 1/50th of a second. Continued practice with magazine covers with low voice and conversational voice in noise. Used skits centering around a grocery store and drug store. Used background noises appropriate for these situations.

Clinical experience as well as controlled research has indicated that the combined approach, stressing the use of lipreading along with auditory training, results in the greatest gains in communication function. The ideal clinical approach incorporates training in both areas so that the individual does not concentrate specifically on lipreading or hearing—he just does his best job of visual listening. If the clinician always remembers that his job is to develop maximum speech perception, and that speech perception means both aural and visual perception, he will be able to have faith in his rehabilitative procedure; if he concentrates on lipreading alone or

FIGURE 13. *Individual child receiving combined auditory and visual stimulation. The hearing aid is being used to maximum benefit.*
(Courtesy American Hearing Society.)

FIGURE 14. *Group auditory-visual stimulation. The children are looking and listening. (Courtesy American Hearing Society.)*

auditory training alone, he will not experience the success for which he hopes.

The authors feel that it is dangerous to specify a method. It is more important to provide the broad frame of a therapeutic approach. The individual therapist can then adapt his approach to the capabilities and behavioral patterns of individual subjects.

Recorded Materials and Listening Test Materials

Sound Effects Records

Speedy-Q-Sound Effects Records, Speedy-Q-Sound Effects, Richmond, Indiana

Major Records—Thomas J. Valentino, Inc., 1600 Broadway, New York, N. Y.

Listening Tests

Brown-Carlsen Listening Comprehension Test. World Book Co., Yonkers-on-Hudson, New York.

Bell Telephone Sentences, in H. Fletcher, and J. C. Steinberg, "Articulation Testing Methods," *Bell System Technical Journal*, 8 (1929), 806-854.

Blewett, Thomas T., "An Experiment in the Measurement of Listening at the College Level." Unpublished doctoral dissertation, University of Missouri, 1945.

Harvard Sentences, in C. V. Hudgins, J. E. Hawkins, J. E. Karlin, and S. S. Stevens, "The Development of Recorded Auditory Tests for Measuring Hearing Loss for Speech," *Laryngoscope* 57 (1947), 57-89.

Nichols, Ralph G., and Leonard A. Stevens, *Are You Listening*. New York: McGraw-Hill Book Co., 1957. Contains many suggestions for the development of tests of listening ability.

Test of Aural Comprehension, Forms A, B and C, English Language Institute, University of Michigan, Ann Arbor, Michigan.

Villarreal, J. J., "A Test of the Aural Comprehension of English for Native Speakers of Spanish," *Speech Monographs,* 15 (1948), 121-132.

7

THE FIRST INSTRUCTION OF LIPREADING INITIATED WITH children, and came about as a by-product associated with teaching young deaf children to speak. Soon it was realized that to complete the communication cycle, the deaf child not only had to learn to express himself orally, but also he had to learn to receive and comprehend oral language used by those about him. This meant concentration upon the visual avenue.

In spite of the fact that lipreading teaching began with children, the Bruhn and Kinzie lipreading methods are the only two well-organized approaches for teaching them. The Jena Method, as published by Bunger, is primarily one for adults, but suggestions are made for adapting it to children. In addition to the published methods there are a few practice materials available, although instructors will soon realize that in order to keep the lessons interesting and meaningful, they will have to create materials themselves.

LIPREADING METHODS AND MATERIALS FOR CHILDREN

In this chapter the methods of Bruhn and Kinzie will be examined and a brief statement will be made about the Jena Method. Pertinent children's materials will be reviewed.

Methods

Bruhn

Martha Bruhn[1] wrote a book of lessons for children based completely on the German Mueller-Walle Method. The principles underlying the lessons are the same as those she set forth in another publication for adults,[2] but the lesson materials are selected and prepared to meet the needs of children. The book is organized so that most visible sounds are presented first and the less visible ones later. Rather than practice on words, emphasis is upon syllables, because syllable practice requires only one mental process, whereas practice on words requires two. (One is recognizing the movements and the second is determining the word those movements represent.) In the forty lessons Bruhn moves directly from rapid drill on syllables to sentence practice. She advocates discussing lipreading with the children before beginning the lessons, thus approaching the situation directly. Each group of sounds studied is carefully examined and at the outset of each lesson, she includes review questions covering the preceding materials. There is a total of 200 questions in the book. Vowels, diphthongs, and consonants are presented separately, then in later lessons combined for syllable practice. Exercises on homonyms and homophenous words are included as a separate section at the end of the book.

Bruhn's method offers an analytical approach, although there is an attempt to get the pupil to see and grasp the whole. Syllables are never to be used alone but always with other ones, unless a particular syllable is described. They must be spoken rapidly and as fluently as running speech. They must not be exaggerated, but always natural. Bruhn advocates that the teacher memorize the syllables to be given and avoid reading from the book. Voice is to be used at all times. The lessons are divided into three parts: (1) Review questions, (2) New lesson materials, and (3) Sentence practice.

[1] M. E. Bruhn, *Elementary Lessons In Lip Reading* (Lynn, Mass., The Nichols Press, 1927).
[2] M. E. Bruhn, *The Mueller-Walle Method of Lipreading for the Hard of Hearing* (Washington, D.C., 1949).

Kinzie

The Kinzies made a unique contribution to the education of hard of hearing and deaf children when they constructed three books of graded lessons in lipreading.[3] The Grade I book contains the simplest approach and consists largely of techniques for developing vocabulary through the use of pictures, objects, and actions. These are enlarged upon until simple sentences within the grasp of the child are developed. The materials for both Grades I and II provide opportunity for self-expression and imagination on the part of the children. The lessons are structured around family life, animals, and other children. They progress systematically from less difficult to more difficult activities. The materials for both Grades I and II link movement and idea at all times. As the Kinzies said ". . . the children are first led into spontaneous, unconscious lipreading, and then step by step, into the more formal instruction which establishes those mental habits and processes that make for subconscious lipreading throughout life." [4]

The Kinzies reasoned that children who come for lipreading instruction realize that objects have names; therefore, the first step in teaching is to make them aware that these names can be discernible on the lips. Rich associations must be made between the objects and the lip movements visible when the names of the objects are spoken. In all, there are 34 lessons in Grade I, and 25 lessons in Grade II. The lessons need not be mastered after one presentation, but they are constructed so that each represents a resource of graded materials which should be mastered before proceeding to the next.

The lessons in Grade II are more highly developed than in Grade I and are referred to as "semi-formal" by the Kinzies. Much attention is devoted to "make-believe" and "imitation." The lessons contain sections with specific movement words, conversational exercises, sentence drills, story exercises, rhymes, and finger play activity. Although no formal explanation of movements is provided, the teacher using the method must draw attention to the formation of sounds as they appear on the lips. In each lesson, different sounds are emphasized and particular words in which these sounds appear

[3] Cora E. Kinzie and Rose Kinzie, *Lip-Reading For Children* (*Grade I, Grade II, Grade III*). (Seattle, Washington, P.O. Box 2044, 1936.)

[4] Cora E. Kinzie and Rose Kinzie, *Lip-Reading For Children, Grade I* (Seattle, Washington, P.O. Box 2044, 1936), p. 2.

are practiced. The conversational exercises are based upon the movement words which are under study. Sentence drills, built upon the movement words, provide a more formal approach to the task. Each child is given the opportunity to repeat many of the sentences as he reads them from the teacher's lips during the lesson. In this area complete mastery is the goal.

The Kinzies state that the story exercise adds interest to the lesson. Each sentence of the story is given to one pupil at a time, to be repeated by him. The entire story is then retold to the group, followed by questions. The rhyme portion of the lesson is also interesting and profitable. Rhymes are said a number of times by the teacher to familiarize the group with them. The teacher may then repeat the rhyme, purposely making an error. By having the children relate the error, the teacher determines how well they were lipreading. Answering questions on the rhyme or repeating it are additional ways suggested by the Kinzies to ascertain the effectiveness of the youngster's learning.

The finger-play activity in Grade II exercises the imagination and holds attention while the child concentrates on the message as it is delivered from the lips of the teacher. The Kinzie's strongly advocate that teachers become thoroughly familiar with the materials before using them so that they can have constant contact with the child. Both Grades I and II are entitled "for children." Grade III is entitled "for juniors."

Through Grades I and II the approach is indirect. However, when the pupil enters Grade III instruction, the lessons are formal. He must now realize that he is working for a specific purpose; and that purpose is to lipread. Preceding the lessons in Grade III, the Kinzies write at some length concerning the fundamental factors to be considered by the instructor of lipreading. Proper grading, use of appropriate materials, and the lesson presentation are points receiving main emphasis. As far as the lessons themselves are concerned, the movement involved is presented by the teacher who writes a description of it on the board. The teacher gives (fullface) the illustrative words to the class. Drills on vocabulary and sentences follow. The story, with its title and important names and words written on the board, is told, and the written words are pointed out as they occur. Nine different techniques for handling the story are suggested by the Kinzies. In all, Grade III contains 45 lessons.

Brauckmann

Karl Brauckmann established a method which he employed with deaf children and adults in Jena, Germany. Translated by Rieghard of the University of Michigan, used by Whitaker at Ypsilanti in 1927, and later published by Bunger,[5] also of Ypsilanti, it was called the Jena Method. This approach, as published by Bunger, is for adults, but throughout the series of lessons there is discussion of how materials can be adapted for deaf and hard of hearing children. A complete discussion of the Jena Method is given in Chapter 8.

Materials

A number of persons who have taught lipreading to children have published books, pamphlets, and films on materials they have found to be useful. They are discussed here as materials because they are not distinctly methods.

Stowell, Samuelson, and Lehman

A. Stowell, E. E. Samuelson, and A. Lehman[6] have written a book directed to the needs of slightly deafened and hard of hearing children. They advocated both the use of words and syllables in practice. For the informal lessons they suggest exercises of lipreading and executing a command the teacher has given, answering questions based on Mother Goose, guessing riddles, and so on. They feel that basic lip movements must be taught and that it is well to compare and contrast these movements with others previously presented.

Whildin and Scally

O. A. Whildin and M. A. Scally[7] have constructed a set of materials for use in teaching speech reading to hard-of-hearing children of the intermediate grades. Even though the term *method* appears in the title, the authors make clear in their introductory remarks that the book does not deal with theory and methods. Its purpose is (1) to present lipreading to the child, and (2) to offer topical information. There are 40 units in all. The first 11 deal with consonants that appear at the beginning of words, the next 24 with vowels, and

---

[5] Anna M. Bunger, *Speech Reading—Jena Method* (Danville, Ill., The Interstate Press, 1952).

[6] A. Stowell, E. Samuelson, and A. Lehman, *Lip Reading For The Deafened Child* (New York: Macmillan Co., 1928).

[7] O. A. Whildin and M. A. Scally, *The Newer Method in Speech Reading For The Hard of Hearing Child* (Westminster: John W. Eckenrode, 1939).

the remaining 5 with combined consonants at the beginnings of words. In general, the units are composed of sentences, stories, and questions. The vocabulary is well suited to children.

Samuelson and Fabregas

E. E. Samuelson and M. B. Fabregas[8] have written an excellent pamphlet in which they present 60 games built around the usage of vocabulary containing sounds of certain classification. The directions are specific and the games can be readily utilized by the lipreading instructor. In selecting the games best suited to the needs of the children, the authors have set up a classified index with six divisions: I. Games Correlated with Other Subjects in the School Curriculum, II. Toy Game, III. Games to Be Used as General Drill on Movements, IV. Miscellaneous Story Games for General Drill, V. Games for Relaxation, and VI. Games Similar to "A Greyhound Bus" or "Spin the Cover." Within division I there is a subject index: (1) Arithmetic, (2) English, (3) Geography, (4) History, (5) Nature, (6) Physical Training, (7) Physiology, and (8) Domestic Science.

New Aids and Materials for Teaching Lipreading

One of the aims of the American Society for the Hard of Hearing, established in 1919, was to encourage the study of lipreading. The book, *New Aids and Materials for Teaching Lip Reading*,[9] was a result of the W.P.A. educational project under the sponsorship of the New York City Board of Education. Written by a committee of project teachers under the guidance of Dr. Edmund P. Fowler and edited by Estelle E. Samuelson, it was given to the American Society for the Hard of Hearing and was published and distributed by them. In writing the manuscript, one purpose was to make available to the elementary school teacher, not trained in lipreading methods, a means by which she could help the accoustically handicapped child. A second purpose was to create, for the trained teacher of lipreading, a book which clarified, supplemented, and organized various aspects of lipreading theory and practice, and presented new and original techniques. The third purpose was to compile practice sentences with their central ideas originating from children.

---

[8] E. E. Samuelson and Minnie B. Fabregas, "A Treasure Chest of Games for Lip Reading Teachers"—Reprint No. 471, *The Volta Bureau*, Washington, D.C., 1939.

[9] *New Aids and Materials for Teaching Lip-Reading* (Washington, D.C.: The American Society for the Hard of Hearing, 1943).

This 169 page book contains five chapters, the first a general manual of instruction for the elementary teachers not trained in lipreading methods. One of the most valuable portions of this first chapter is in the formal, informal, correlation, and introductory lessons presented. The authors have been careful to make each step in the lesson clear so that the interested but untrained teacher can easily understand the procedures involved.

Chapter 2 is devoted to a discussion and actual presentation of some new techniques and theory to be utilized by trained teachers of lipreading. The visibility chart developed by the authors is excellent. Each sound of English has been assigned a constant numerical value. For example, the sound [b], as in ball, is highly visible and thus has a visibility value of 1. The [ng] sound is not visible and thus has a value of 0. With this guide, the teacher can carefully grade each sound, syllable, word, or sentence she constructs for practice material. Both Chapters 1 and 2 make up Part I of the text which is referred to as the "Theory" portion of the book. Part II is labeled "Materials."

There are four chapters in Part II, that is 3, 4, 5, and 6. Chapter 3 deals with consonants, Chapter 4 with vowels, Chapter 5 with diphthongs, and Chapter 6 with picture sentences. In Chapters 3, 4, and 5, descriptions of sounds, word drills, and tested sentences are provided. Chapter 6 gives sentences that can be used with pictures to serve as the basis of an informal lesson.

Beginning Lip Reading

Leavis[10] published a book of lessons and exercises in lipreading for teachers of children in the first three grades. In the preparation of the lesson, she includes teaching of sound movements, exercises for bodily activity, and materials helpful to the child in his regular classroom work. Leavis points out that lessons should close on a happy note so that the youngsters look forward to returning to their lipreading class.

Yenrick

Yenrick,[11] in 1951, discussed materials selected from units of study commonly used in the primary grades. He says that regular classroom

---

[10] May H. Leavis, *Beginning Lip Reading* (386 Commonwealth Ave., Boston 15, Mass., 1949).

[11] D. E. Yenrick, "Speechreading Materials for the Primary Public School Grades," *The Volta Review* (June 1951), Reprint No. 625.

materials can be adapted for lipreading lessons. After analyzing five primary books, he showed how various parts of each could be adapted for speech reading purposes.

In a later publication, Yenrick[12] presented a variety of lessons correlated with activities of children in grades four through eight. He demonstrated how classroom topics could be worked into the speech reading lesson.

Hearing With Our Eyes

Ena Macnutt[13] makes clear that she is not presenting a method, but a set of lessons to be utilized by teachers who are seeking new materials. The early lessons are based upon highly visible movements. Each of the lessons has sufficient materials for 30 to 45 minutes of work and contains 24 sentences, a story, and two games or devices. The lessons become progressively more difficult. Macnutt advocates the use of voice. A rather unique aspect of the Macnutt materials is the workbook[14] that accompanies the text. Properly employed, the workbook is a means by which pupil progress can be followed.

Stories and Games for Easy Lipreading Practice

Feilbach,[15] realizing the need for interesting material in lipreading practice, compiled a book of games and stories. Although the material in the book can be used successfully with children in as low as the third grade, the book was also prepared for adolescents and adults.

Morkovin and Moore

In addition to their original films for classroom use, Morkovin and Moore[16] created a new series of Life Situation films for children. There are five 5-minute black-and-white sound films in the set: (1) "Tommy's Table Manners," (2) "A Lesson In Magic," (3) "The Little Cowboy," (4) "Barbara's New Shoes," and (5) "Bow Belinda."

[12] D. E. Yenrick, "Speech Reading Materials," *Hearing News* (September 1951), Reprint No. 246.
[13] Ena G. Macnutt, *Hearing With Our Eyes* (175 Dartmouth St., Boston 16, Mass., 1952).
[14] Ena G. Macnutt, *Lipreading Workbook To Accompany Hearing With Our Eyes* (175 Dartmouth St., Boston 16, Mass., 1952).
[15] Rose V. Feilbach, *Stories and Games for Easy Lipreading Practice* (Washington, D.C., The Volta Bureau, 1952).
[16] B. V. Morkovin and Lucellia Moore, *Life Situation Films*, 16mm. sound films, set of five (Department of Cinema, University of Southern California, University Park, Los Angeles 7, California).

Morkovin[17] points out that the films are structured around incidents interesting to children, and advocates the use of hearing aids for success. One objective in showing the films is to re-enforce life experiences and activities and to facilitate the aurally handicapped child's language approach to them. Another is to help the child achieve greater fluency in speech and speech reading. A third is to provide the child, through exercises, the opportunity to make precise discrimination of visual, auditory, kinesthetic, tactile, and rhythmic aspects of oral language.

Whitehurst

Whitehurst[18] combined, in a manual, auditory training, lipreading, and speech. The author views her materials as supplementary to those used in basic courses for auditory rehabilitation. The lessons are structured for children 12 to 16 years of age. Whitehurst presents 14 units in which vocabulary building, auditory training, lipreading, and speech are presented through a travelogue. The pupil has a workbook in which he writes responses to the many varied activities presented by the teacher. This approach represents a real attempt to integrate vocabulary building, auditory training, lipreading, and speech, which are so important to the aurally handicapped.

[17] Boris V. Morkovin, "Participation of the Hearing Impaired Child in Life Situations," *Better Hearing* (Spring 1957).

[18] Mary W. Whitehurst, *Let's Travel*, Teacher's Manual and Pupils Workbook (Hearing Rehabilitation, 1072 North Drive, East Meadow, N.Y., 1958).

8

SOON AFTER LIPREADING INSTRUCTION WAS ESTABLISHED for children, there was sufficient demand for classes structured specifically for adults. As a result, a number of well defined adult methods were developed by such leaders as Nitchie, Kinzie, Bruhn, and Brauckmann. Many others, however, contributed lesson materials for adults without setting forth a particular set of rules. Still others, in effect, combined aspects of several established methods. It is the purpose of this chapter to review and compare the adult methods of Nitchie, Kinzie, Bruhn, and Brauckmann as well as other outstanding adult lesson materials.

Methods

Nitchie

Edward B. Nitchie[1] published several books stating the basic principles that he thought were involved in the

---

[1] E. B. Nitchie, *Lip-Reading, Principles and Practice* (New York: Frederick A. Stokes Company, 1912).

LIPREADING METHODS AND MATERIALS FOR ADULTS

lipreading act, as well as methods by which to employ those principles in teaching. His most famous contribution was his last book, published in 1912. Elizabeth H. Nitchie, his widow, has since revised the book on several occasions after his death in 1917. In 1940, Mrs. Nitchie[2] published a series of lessons in lipreading based upon the fundamentals of the system established by her husband.

At the start Nitchie advocated an analytical approach to lipreading, but he saw that he was in error and began to instruct his pupils to synthesize what they read. He realized that when they tried to understand "the whole" rather than one part at a time, they were much more successful. He advocated practice, but warned that the wrong kind could do more harm than good. Nitchie[3] set forth the following principles that he felt were essential to the teaching of lipreading: (1) Be natural, (2) be thorough, (3) make the work interesting, (4) lose no opportunities, (5) guard against methods that may interfere with the development of any desirable habit, and (6) seek to meet the peculiar needs of each pupil.

In order to apply the principles, certain methods in the training of the eye and the mind were necessary. For the eye training, Nitchie suggested that accuracy could be developed through practice with lists of words and sentences in which only one word or movement is changed from sentence to sentence. Mirror practice also was recommended. Mouthing and exaggeration were considered of little value. His method for the training of visual memory was built around the "movement words" presented in each lesson. For example, in the lesson for [L], some of his movement words included [she, thee, lee], [teach, teeth, deal], [shed, then, let], [edge, eth, ell]. Students were given the opportunity to compare and contrast the other movements with the [L], and, in time, subconscious knowledge of the movements involved in lipreading was developed.

For mind training, which Nitchie thought extremely important, he emphasized synthesization and not word for word accuracy. He believed that understanding the words from the thought was more important than the thought from the words. Whether the unit be a short sentence, groups of sentences, or stories, stress should always be placed upon the whole rather than parts. Development of intuitive power was also emphasized. His technique was to tell the pupil a familiar story and then retell it, adding many details. The pupil was

---

[2] Elizabeth H. Nitchie, *New Lessons in Lip-Reading* (Philadelphia: J. B. Lippincott Company, 1940).

[3] E. B. Nitchie, "Teaching Lip-Reading," *The Volta Review*, 18 (1916), p. 276.

then given questions to answer concerning the story. Still another way to develop intuitiveness was to present the student with a practice word that he understood and then immediately follow with a sentence containing the word. Another method was to present the student several sentences, one after another, each associated in thought. Homophenous words, colloquial forms, conversion practice, and informal lectures were suggested as useful ways to exercise intuitive powers. For developing quickness of mind, Nitchie suggested that a rapid response be made by the pupils. For alertness of mind, he stressed rapid identification of words and sentences. Finally, for securing the pupils concentration, the work should be interesting and varied.

Through his principles, Nitchie emphasized the importance of teachers attending to the motor as well as the visible language form. In his lessons he always introduced the sound or group of sounds he was about to teach. The Introduction explains how the sounds were made and their relationship to other sounds.

Bruhn

The basis of the Bruhn[4] method was rapid, rhythmic, syllable drills. Since the syllable is the basic unit of the words that comprise sentences, it should be subconsciously recognized. Bruhn's aims were not unlike those of Nitchie. She felt that the pupil should learn to (1) feel the sound sensations of speech, (2) observe carefully, and (3) be alert and quick to perceive the rapid movements of speech. As did Nitchie, Bruhn conceived of lipreading as a training of the eye and mind. Grasping the whole rather than parts was stressed. However, she did suggest that analytic fixating was needed for grasping details; the eye, in taking the place of the ear, must be thoroughly trained to distinguish the visible characteristics of the movements of the speech organs.

In working with syllables, Bruhn stressed the necessity of never using one syllable alone except when explaining the movements associated with it. She further advised that in the construction of syllable drills, there should be contrast in the direction of the movement of the syllables. The rhythmic aspect of the syllables must also be considered. One syllable of a group should be carried over to the following group. In giving the syllable drills, she cautioned the

[4] Martha E. Bruhn, *The Mueller-Walle Method of Lipreading for the Hard of Hearing* (Washington, D.C.: 1949).

teacher against exaggeration and syllable separation. Properly given, they should glide into each other, and the students should take them as fast as possible. Drills must be repeated until the lipreader can recognize them subconsciously. The very obscure movements can be drilled in sentences.

Bruhn felt that the study of lipreading involved visual, auditory, and motor memory. Visual-minded persons, she thought, tend to be analytical, whereas auditory-minded persons participate in lipreading since it involves articulatory sensations which are a part of speech.

Bruhn's plans for lessons are divided into four parts. The first is definition of the movement or movements of the new sound to be studied. These movements are contrasted with the ones previously studied, and are presented by the teacher from various angles. The second part of the lesson consists of written work; the third, a brief story or talk, and the fourth is devoted to group practice or a question period. The lesson is to be given with voice at all times.

Kinzie

The method of Cora and Rose Kinzie[5] represents a blend of principles and practices set forth by both Nitchie and Bruhn. From Nitchie they adopted the psychological approach to lipreading and also his method of using practice words and sentence building. From Bruhn, which was in essence, Mueller-Walle, they adopted the introductory classification of sounds. The Kinzies then constructed a series of graded lesson materials for children and adults. They felt that material which is too difficult discourages, and that which is too easy is not challenging; in either instance, satisfactory development of speech reading power does not occur. They graded lesson materials so that individual students could progress from one level of attainment to the next, and in time achieve maximum skill. The graded materials for both adults and children are built upon the same word list, and the movements in each of the grades are presented in the same order. Therefore, the adult pupil could move from one level or grade to another, and yet work within a framework of the same procedure. Grading of words, sentences, and stories was the outstanding characteristic of the Kinzie materials.

In the construction of sentences, the Kinzies laid down specific guiding principles. First of all, the sentence should be *definite* such

[5] Cora E. Kinzie and Rose Kinzie, *Lip-Reading For The Deafened Adult* (Chicago: John C. Winston Co., 1931).

as, "The baby's shoe is on the sofa," not indefinite as "It was the least possible." The Kinzies reasoned that indefinite sentences have no distinguishing characteristics and therefore do not give the pupil a fair chance to employ his intuitive and synthetic processes. They reasoned that sentences should be natural in their structure as well as language. Natural sentences resemble those used in conversation. Inverted sentences, with phrases or clauses appearing at the beginning, would be classed as unnatural, such as, "Encouraged by their success, the army renewed their attack." However, if the introductory clause contains highly visible sounds or the clue word of the sentence, the Kinzies considered it to be acceptable. Word selection should also be natural. "The boy is as tall as his father," is far better than the unnatural sentence, "The boy's height is equal to that of his father." They asserted that sentences must be *interesting, pleasing,* and *rhythmic.* Pleasing sentences are in all instances interesting, but interesting sentences are not necessarily pleasing. Rhythmic sentences are those characterized by a regular beat or harmonious recurrence of stress. A final requirement is that all sentences be *dignified.*

In story selection, the Kinzies considered the short, humorous story to have the greatest value for beginners and intermediates. They also suggested good stories concerning famous people as excellent materials for these two levels. For the advanced levels, however, they advised utilization of choice literary selections.

A synthetic approach to lipreading is stressed by the Kinzies, as well as mirror practice and the use of voice. In their lessons, movements associated with sound production are explained, illustrative words given, and sometimes contrast words are presented. A vocabulary list precedes the work on sentences. In the more advanced lessons, stories, and questions concerning the stories are furnished. Included in the work they structured for adults are 36 lessons on sound movements, 36 lessons on stories, and 18 lessons devoted to homophenous words.

Brauckmann

Bessie Whitaker and Anna Bunger were responsible for introducing the method of the German, Karl Brauckmann, to hard of hearing adults in the United States. It is referred to as the Jena method. In her text, *Speech Reading—Jena Method,* Bunger[6] outlined an appli-

---

[6] Anna M. Bunger, *Speech Reading—Jena Method* (Danville, Ill.: The Interstate Press, 1952).

cation of Brauckmann's method. The method emphasizes the syllable and rhythm and the forms of speech (audible, visible, movement, mimetic and gesture). Brauckmann thought of the movement form as being complete for everyone who speaks, and the audible form as complete for anyone regardless of his status of hearing, for only fragments of the movement form are available to any who attempt to view muscular movements associated with speech. The mimetic form is viewed as incomplete but extremely important. Gesture form is not complete but this visible phenomenon gives emphasis to the other forms.

Bunger stated that the first aim of the student of speech reading is to develop awareness of the movements of speech and to learn how these movements feel. This is called *kinesthesis*. Kinesthetic awareness soon becomes a substitute for auditory awareness.

Since the primary emphasis is on syllables, Bunger explained their formation and composition. The syllable is composed of vowels and consonants which are formed by shaping movements of the vowels and articulatory movements of the consonants. The student must be concerned with only three parts of articulation, the lip, tongue and palate. The consonants are presented and classified under headings: (1) Lips, (2) Tongue, and (3) Tongue-Soft Palate. The vowels (a, e, i, o, u) are also presented. For practice, the consonants should be combined with vowels and said aloud rapidly by the teacher as the hard of hearing student follows suit. The student is asked, each time he says them aloud, to attend to the port of articulation involved in the production of the syllables. Upon locating the proper port, the student enters the sound combination under the correct category, that is, lips, tongue or tongue-soft palate. Teacher and student can say the syllables together with certain rhythms as la–la–la–la–la, or perhaps ka–ka–ka. The consonant classifications in the Jena Method are:

Lips	Tongue	Tongue-Soft-Palate
b	d	g
p	t	k
v	z–zh–j	y
f	s–sh–ch	
m	n	ng–rk
w	r	
wh	th (thin)	h
	th (father)	
	l	

The student is also asked to memorize this series of vowels:

a – name	e – met	i – ice
e – we	oo – soon	oi – oil
o – go	a – at	oo – look
a – far	u – cube	i – this
a – ball	ow – town	u – up

Memorization of the vowel order is the only rote learning required of the student who makes use of this method.

In order to emphasize the rhythmic aspect of the syllable drill, Bunger suggested that a basic rhythm pattern be established to accompany the drill by employing some bodily movement such as clapping, tapping, or ball bouncing. The pattern is preset and students follow in unison. Thus a group might tap a pattern utilizing stressed ($\perp$) and unstressed ($\smile$) components in the following manner: [$\perp \smile \perp \smile \perp \smile \perp \smile \perp \perp \perp$]. Syllables are uttered as the tapping or bouncing of balls proceeds. The components of the syllables are identified at the end of each exercise. Then the entire list of vowels may be used with a consonant in the rhythm developed.

In theory, the accented syllables of normal speech provide the rhythms of speech, and thus a cue to the speech reader. The aims in practicing rhythmic exercises in unison are to alert the student to the feeling of speech movement as he talks, to teach him to imitate visible speech movements as he watches another talk, and to practice fundamental rhythmic exercises that are consistent with the contrasting movements and stressed syllables of the oral language, so that he is learning something which is applicable to the speech reading task.

A typical exercise to increase speech reading proficiency through strengthening the visual, auditory, and motor pathways is a number series such as 1–2–3–4–5–6–7–8–9–10–9–8–7–6–5–4–3–2–1. The teacher speaks the numbers out of order, and the students attempt to follow. This can be done also with days of the week, months of the year, and so on.

Three types of materials used in the Jena Method are (1) syllable exercises, (2) grammatical forms, and (3) conversation and stories. Stress is laid upon the syllable drills in the early lessons and application made of these drills in word series.

Summary of Methods

Each of the leading methods is somewhat different but there is greater similarity than difference among them. In the four major methods presented, all advocate a face to face approach in lipreading practice, and all emphasize synthesis on the part of the student. Although Bruhn and Brauckmann stress careful analysis of phonetic components, the work is primarily directed on grasping wholes. Bruhn, Nitchie, Brauckmann, and the Kinzies all stress the utilization of the auditory sense to the fullest extent, as well as the importance of visual and motor reinforcement. Brauckmann particularly emphasizes rhythm practice, and Nitchie and Kinzie find individual teaching desirable. The "mouthing" of speech to pupils is not recommended, but all suggest the use of voice by the teacher in practice. It is interesting to note that the materials of the four leading methods consist of individual words, sentences, and stories. Bruhn and Brauckmann, however, stress practice with the syllable.

Although it is well for the student to use one particular method with skill, it is also desirable for him to adopt the best aspects from each method, thereby profiting from an eclectic approach. There are no objective research results available that show any one method to be superior to the others.

Materials

Many others interested in lipreading instruction have compiled materials to make the teaching and learning more systematic and interesting. This section will present a study of materials helpful to the busy clinician or teacher who wishes to select them for use.

Morgenstern

The book by Louise I. Morgenstern[7] is now over 40 years old, but contains many lessons and exercises that are still used successfully. The book is divided into three parts. Following a general introduction to the topic of lipreading, an outline of suggestions for lesson planning, and hints to the pupil, Morgenstern presents Part I which consists of 22 lessons. The lessons, in turn, are divided into three sections. The first section, devoted to the study of specific sounds,

[7] Louise I. Morgenstern, *Lip-Reading for Class Instruction* (New York: Noble and Noble Publishers, 1916).

contains drill and contrast words. The second section includes practice words incorporating the sounds under study. The third section is directed toward sentence practice, and contains the words previously employed in section two. Part II of the book is devoted to consonant combinations. The 19 lessons include practice lists of words and sentences and homophenous words, common phrases, conversational sentences, and dictation practice. Practice stories and dialogues appear in Part III. Morgenstern advocates the synthetic approach by the way her materials are assembled.

Mason

Marie Mason[8] outlined a course of instruction in visual hearing based upon a series of 30 sixteen millimeter silent color films. Each film is approximately eight minutes long and is a complete instructional unit. The sequence of the 30 films proceeds from the easier to the more difficult aspects of visual hearing. Each film is composed of three parts. The first, functioning as a text, announces the topic, and shows several cards upon which sentences are printed for the student to read before the filmed speaker utters them. In the second part, the speaker recites the remainder of the script. The third part consists of questions directed toward the student concerning the material covered in the lesson. Most of the sentences given in the films are unrelated. Mason felt that this develops alertness in making visual discriminations, and provides a background of visual memory of the sounds. In each sentence, there is a specific consonant sound that is frequently repeated. In order to give practice in synthesizing, some of the film scripts present related sentences, and others contain discussions of a particular topic. Films V, X, XX and XXX review the materials in the films preceding them, and can well be utilized as test films.

Mason was not attempting to replace the clinician with her film, but wanted to supplement the work of the teacher and to provide instruction in the areas where skilled assistance was not available. At the time of her death in 1950, she had completed a portion of the manuscript on Visual Hearing that was to serve as a manual to be used with her films. (For a complete description of the content of the Mason Visual Hearing Films see Appendix B.)

[8] Marie K. Mason, *Visual Hearing—A Method of Teaching the Visual Comprehension of Speech* (Unpublished Manual, Columbus, Ohio: The Ohio State University, n.d.).

Montague

Harriet Montague[9] constructed a useful book of thirty lessons for the beginning adult lipreader. It contains helpful suggestions not only for the lipreader, but also for the person who is to conduct the practice sessions, and for the teacher of lipreading. The lessons presented are based upon Montague's experience in teaching beginning adult lipreaders. The movements employed follow those used in the Mueller-Walle Method of lipreading. Each lesson contains words, phrases, sentences, and stories and each utilizes a set of movements. As the lessons progress, they become increasingly difficult.

The Deshon Book

The material in the lipreading practice book[10] written at Deshon General Hospital consists of contributions made by the teachers of the Lip Reading Section of the Aural Rehabilitation Service. Subjects of the lessons are biography, games, geography, history, humor, personality, general information, and miscellaneous. This material is useful to the clinician responsible for adults in individual or group classes. Here no one particular method is discussed for it is simply a book of practice materials.

Morkovin and Moore

Boris Morkovin and Lucelia Moore[11] constructed a set of films for use with both adults and children. The real purpose underlying the Morkovin-Moore films is to provide a method where students in the classroom can practice lipreading in lifelike situations. They did not feel that drill upon syllables or disconnected phrases, with no relation to life situations, should be used.[12] According to Morkovin and Moore, a primary goal in speech reading training is for the student to grasp the situation quickly, and make meaningful the nonverbal as well as verbal clues.

[9] Harriet Montague, *Lip Reading Lessons For Adult Beginners* (Washington, D.C.: The Volta Bureau, 1945).

[10] Barbara Ferguson, and eds., *The Deshon Book of Lip Reading Practice Material* (Washington, D.C.: The Volta Bureau, 1946).

[11] Boris V. Morkovin and Lucelia M. Moore, *"A Contextual-Synthetic Approach For Speech Reading," Life Situation Motion Pictures* (Mimeographed Manual, 1949).

[12] B. V. Morkovin, "Rehabilitation of the Aurally Handicapped Through the Study of Speech Reading in Life Situations," *Journal of Speech and Hearing Disorders*, 12 (1947), 363-368.

The films have been constructed to train the student to:

1. derive meaning from context,
2. distinguish details through the synesthetic approach (co-operation of audio-visual-kinesthetic senses), and
3. recognize details subconsciously.

As with Mason, Morkovin and Moore do not attempt to minimize the role of the teacher with their films, but provide the teacher with a tool by which lipreading can be made more effective. Morkovin[13] suggests that the teacher run and re-run the films, then return to words that are not understood, and separate the more difficult ones into parts. The teacher can carry out choric speech activities by having the students read aloud the lips of the film characters.

The Morkovin-Moore films are ten in number and present such situations as "The Family Dinner," "At The Bank," and the like. Certain sounds are stressed in each film. A manual accompanies the films and contains eight hours of detailed lesson plans for each film, along with the complete dialogues.

Ordman and Ralli

Kathryn Ordman and Mary Ralli[14] presented the Nitchie School basic course in lipreading. Their object was to reproduce everyday conversations as closely as possible. In the introduction the authors set forth rules for increasing lipreading effectiveness:

1. Concentrate on the thought expressed, not on individual words.
2. Do not interrupt a speaker to ask him to repeat. Sometimes the entire meaning will be grasped from the last words spoken.
3. Watch the speaker's mouth constantly.

Lipreading and hearing aid, angles and distance, background noise, training in listening, auditory training and feeling, and rhythm of speech are all discussed briefly. There are 30 lessons. The first three contain introductory lipreading material consisting of simple associated sentences. In lessons 4 through 20, the fundamental movements of English speech are presented. One consonant movement is considered in each lesson, whereas the vowels are studied in groups of three. The last nine lessons are devoted to consonant combinations.

[13] Morkovin, *ibid.*, p. 365.
[14] Kathryn A. Ordman and Mary P. Ralli, *What People Say* (New York: The Nitchie School of Lip Reading, Inc., mimeographed, 1949).

Faircloth

M. Faircloth[15] dedicated her booklet of lipreading practice material to the Canadians who had returned deafened from World War II. In each of the 23 lessons there is a section devoted to general discussions of the problems involved in lipreading. A second section considers the study and practice of syllables, conversational topics, and sentences. Following this is advice on how to practice.

Faircloth suggests that students learn the vowels as arranged by Brauckmann, and presents the consonants as originally proposed by E. B. Nitchie. Faircloth's primary objective is to teach students to improve memory of speech experience and to learn to feel oral sensations. She suggests that oral sensations contribute to speech memory and are made possible through utilization of the auditory, kinesthetic, and visual pathways.

Feilbach

The practice booklet prepared by Rose Feilbach[16] does not express a method or a point of view. Humorous stories abound and are followed by questions. This little volume contains 68 games, quizzes and pupil readings, 23 true stories and legends, and 9 anecdotes. These materials have been successfully employed by Feilbach not only with adults but also with junior and senior high school students.

Fisher

Mae Fisher[17] constructed a practice book of lipreading to be used with teenagers and adults. There are 25 different exercises in all. Some are structured around important people and places as well as around numbers and particular words. The exercises are stimulating and challenging.

Ewing

In her book *Lipreading and Hearing Aids,*[18] Ewing presents two excellent courses of lipreading designated as Course A—12 lessons, and Course B—8 lessons. Course A is for the beginner, whereas

[15] M. Faircloth, *Lip Reading Study and Practice* (Toronto: The Ryerson Press, 1946).

[16] Rose V. Feilbach, *Stories and Games for Easy Lipreading Practice* (Washington, D.C.: The Volta Bureau, 1952).

[17] Mae T. Fisher, *Let's Practice Lipreading!* (Washington, D.C.: The Volta Bureau, 1957).

[18] I. R. Ewing, *Lipreading and Hearing Aids* (Manchester, England, Manchester University Press, 1959), pp. 45-73.

Course B is for the student who has gained some lipreading skill. Lessons in Course A are directed toward visually familiarizing the student with highly predictable language units, rhythm of speech, and the phonetic components that make up words, phrases, and sentences. Attention is also directed to the sounds which begin words as well as those which end words.

The Course B is composed of lessons that contain practice materials and procedures for helping the student to understand more rapid speech. Complicated sentences are introduced as well as dialogue practice. One lesson is devoted to practice under difficult lipreading conditions, for example when shadows are on the face of the speaker and when the speaker is walking about the room.

9

RATHER THAN OUTLINING A SERIES OF LESSONS OR DISCUSS-
ing various methods of lipreading instruction, this chapter will express a viewpoint regarding the management
of the aurally handicapped.

Traditionally, the teaching of lipreading has been
approached like other academic subjects. Writers of lesson plans have emphasized starting with certain sounds
and movements and progressing through a series of exercises until all the ground has been covered. In doing
this it was hoped that the acoustically handicapped person would become proficient in the art of lipreading.
As could be expected, several different approaches to
the teaching of lipreading have evolved.

In spite of the merit of formal lipreading lessons, the
authors feel that the best approach in management of
the acoustically handicapped is the individualized one.
No two aurally handicapped persons are alike, and
therefore the needs of each differ. Even though the long-

AN APPROACH TO PLANNING OF
LIPREADING LESSONS

range goals of the lipreading teacher will be the same for a number of persons—teaching them all to lipread—the intermediate goals will vary greatly. It is these intermediate or specific goals with which the teacher of lipreading is concerned daily. The procedures used to attain the specific goals are dictated by the status of the acoustically handicapped person, that is, how well he can lipread, how severely he is handicapped, how motivated he is to do something about his condition, how willing he is to face his problem, his age, his occupation, et cetera. This information comes only as the handicapped person is tested and interviewed, or in the case of children, as parents are interviewed. In other words, each person must be dealt with individually, and in terms of individual needs. This is not to say that all lipreading training must be carried out individually, for in most instances group work is indicated; but in the group work an attempt must be made to provide each individual with the kind of materials and practice he needs. Carefully planned lessons can accomplish this.

Presented below are brief accounts of twelve persons, all with acoustic handicaps, but with different needs.

Cases and Discussion

Case 1. Mrs. X, an alert 62-year-old wife of a wealthy retired business executive, has a slight loss of hearing. Hearing evaluation shows that her loss is 25 decibels in both ears throughout the speech range. Otological reports reveal that neither medication nor surgical intervention is indicated. The loss is one which is characterized by inner ear malfunction. Mrs. X has undergone hearing aid evaluation but does not profit sufficiently from an aid to justify the purchase of one. She has considerable difficulty in discriminating sounds with similar acoustic characteristics. Of late, Mrs. X has found it increasingly difficult to follow conversation in a group. In a face to face situation with one person she has little trouble lipreading. However, when a speaker's head is turned slightly in talking to another, Mrs. X finds it difficult to follow what is said. Most of her group activity is in the women's clubs or charity groups with which she is affiliated. Mrs. X is poised, has confidence in herself, and gives evidence of being psychologically mature. She is able to verbalize her problem clearly. She came of her own accord to the clinic to seek specialized help in learning to lipread better.

In planning the lessons for this handicapped woman, it was necessary here, as it is in every instance, to start working on those individual problems that were most troublesome. With Mrs. X it was not a matter of convincing her to learn to lipread, for she knew how, but was seeking help in becoming more proficient; it was not a matter of helping her rebuild her self-concept, for she was poised and mature; it was not a matter of encouraging her to participate in more social groups, for she was an active member of several; it was not a matter of methodically teaching her movements involved in speech sound production, for she was already a good lipreader. Mrs. X had two troublesome problems upon which attention was focused. One was in discriminating sounds of speech and the other was in lipreading conversation within a group. Therefore, the training was directed toward speech sound discrimination and reading the lips of speakers as their faces were placed at an angle rather than full face. Time devoted to controlled conversational practice in a group was also considered as an important part of the training for Mrs. X.

Case 2. Mr. Y, a 34-year-old machinist had been losing his hearing for the past ten years. At present, his average loss through the frequencies important for hearing speech is 58 decibels. His loss is almost the same in both ears. He has recently been evaluated for a hearing aid and has acquired one. His aided speech reception threshold is 36 decibels, but he still has considerable difficulty in speech sound discrimination and is far from convinced that training of any kind might be beneficial. He has gradually withdrawn from social situations that demand his participation in conversation. In addition, he finds the task of lipreading a difficult one.

A different approach to therapy planning took place for Mr. Y than for Mrs. X. because their specific needs were not alike, even though the long-range goals (teaching them to become more proficient lipreaders) were the same. Mr. Y was led to an understanding of the importance of aural rehabilitation for purposes of better social adjustment. Even though his aid was benefiting him greatly, he received concentrated work in auditory training in order to learn to utilize his residual hearing and his hearing aid more effectively. He also was given training in lipreading which was very basic and elementary at the outset.

Case 3. Twelve-year-old Brenda has worn an aid for six years. She has a moderate loss of hearing but with help from teachers, parents, and the speech and hearing therapist she has made excellent social adjustment and her scholastic performance has consistently been a little above the average of her class. She has several hobbies and is an active Girl Scout. She has two younger sisters and an older brother. Brenda is a happy child and enjoys coming to the clinic for instruction in lipreading and auditory training. She is very co-operative with her therapist. She does an average job of lipreading but is in need of continued training.

The approach to lesson planning for Brenda was not difficult. Her primary need was continued practice in lipreading. She profited from work in a small group of four other children whose needs were very similar to hers. Individual instruction in lipreading or auditory training was not necessary. The real challenge was to provide interesting lessons, the materials of which were well suited to the age level of the class in which Brenda was enrolled.

Case 4. Bobbie, a four-year-old boy, was recently discovered to be hard of hearing. His parents had been baffled by his behavior since he was 2½ years old, at which time he had scarlet fever. The reason they came to the clinic was to discover if Bobbie could be taught to "talk better." It was at this time that his hearing problem was revealed. Bobbie had learned some speech before the onset of his hearing loss. At the present time, however, many of his speech attempts are unintelligible. The youngest of five children, Bobbie has been looked upon as the baby of the family and has been spoiled by having his own way most of the time. As far as can be determined, his hearing loss would be classified as severe. His speech attempts consist mainly of uttering nouns. Occasionally he tries to say what sounds like *go, do* and *give.* He is extremely deficient in the use of oral language, especially perception and expression. Currently, his parents are enrolling him in a special school for the acoustically handicapped.

In order to make lipreading instruction meaningful, Bobbie had to learn to attend to the activities which were set up for him. When first taken into therapy, he did not understand that he was there to work, and moved as he pleased about the room, playing with any and all toys that attracted his attention. Thus in the beginning, the specific goal was to teach him to sit in one chair and attend to the activities prepared for him. Certainly, at this point, emphasis was not on lipreading. Once he learned to concentrate, however, attention was directed toward teaching him some language. Basic language building activities were structured which aided the expansion of his vocabulary. He related what he saw on the lips of the therapist with pictures and objects. Soon his vocabulary had increased considerably. He also learned to watch carefully the faces of those about him who were speaking. Here was a child in need of lipreading training, but in need of a great deal more than just lipreading. The long-range goal for this child was to establish adequate utilization of oral language. To reach his goal meant (1) continued work in language training, (2) auditory training, (3) lipreading instruction, and (4) speech therapy.

Case 5. Shirley is 20 years old and a junior in college. She has a hearing level which averages between 50-55 decibels in each ear through the frequencies that are important for understanding speech. She has sustained this loss since early childhood. Shirley has a hearing aid but refuses to wear it except when forced to do so. She jokes a great deal and attempts to radiate self-assurance. It is difficult for her to hear her professors, and as a result she depends largely upon copying lecture notes from her classmates. She spends an inordinate amount of time preparing for her lessons. Currently, she is enrolled for group and individual therapy. When group discussion periods are directed toward problems of adjustment faced by the acoustically handicapped, she becomes un-co-operative and somewhat belligerent. Up to this point she refuses to admit that she has a problem, although she does admit that she has been penalized socially "for some reason or other." Her lipreading ability is only fair and her oral expressive language performance is average to below average. She becomes disturbed when this deficiency is made evident. Articulation of [r, s, z] is deviant. Shirley prefers individual sports and spare time activities that can be carried out alone. She is quite attractive and well groomed, but for the most part she is seen alone around the campus.

Shirley has many problems, but if she could lipread with proficiency the arduous task of preparing her lessons would be much easier. Therefore, increased lipreading ability should be among the first considerations. Also of primary importance is continued work on helping her recognize her handicaps and evaluating them herself. This should contribute to her greater happiness, not only in the present but in the future. Instead of purposely shunning social groups, Shirley should learn to cope with her communication handicap, and objectively evaluate reactions of others toward her. The importance of using a hearing aid must be stressed. Where refusal to wear the aid is as pronounced as it is with Shirley, there is real cause for re-evaluating it. Perhaps it is not working properly, or it may not give adequate amplification. After it has been established that her aid, or another one, is the one she should wear, then auditory training should be given with the aid in position. Her language and articulation problems are secondary. These should receive systematic attention, but only after the previously mentioned problems are under control.

Case 6. Susan is only three and a half years old and had already had the equivalent of a year of aural habilitation before being brought to the Speech and Hearing Clinic. As a result of preliminary otological and audiological evaluations, Susan was fitted with an aid and placed in a pre-school nursery group of hard of hearing children. She has participated in language building activities and has had incidental training in lipreading. She has an expressive vocabulary of about 50 words but is able to comprehend many more. She is alert and co-operative and participates well in examination and therapy periods. Due to successful play audiometric procedures employed during six different testing sessions, it was determined that her bone conduction threshold was normal. This called for further otological study, the result of which was the discovery of a middle-ear anomaly. The medical consultants feel reasonably certain that the present condition can be altered, and if so, hearing restored to normalcy. It is understood by the parents, however, that the operation would be of an exploratory nature, and the outcome might not be successful in terms of restored hearing. The otologists have recommended that the parents discuss with the audiologist in charge of Susan's habilitative program, the prognosis as regards speech development, school placement, and progress if she continues to live with the present handicap.

Although Susan was brought to the clinic for lipreading and speech training, careful assessment of her individual needs, in attempting to structure a tailored program, led to problems far more basic to Susan at this time than lipreading and speech. True, the long-range goal is to help Susan communicate effectively, but the specific goals are not speech and lipreading practice. Rather, the immediate need is to help Susan's parents get a realistic picture of their child's progress against a background of norms for children with normal hearing. In addition, they must be given as true a picture as possible of the effect of hearing loss on scholastic achievement, social adjustment, and vocational placement. If, after they have pondered the situation, they decide to go through with the operation, they should be given full psychological support. They should also be reassured that if the operation yields no better hearing for Susan, the habilitation program will be resumed in the Speech and Hearing Clinic with only a few weeks lost.

Case 7. Ann is 23 years old and deafened. She lost her hearing when she was 4 years of age. She is superior in lipreading; however, her speech is at times quite difficult to understand. She is a college graduate and presently enrolled as a graduate student. Her academic record is well above average, and she is intensively interested in her professional future. She has had aural rehabilitation for approximately four years, and feels that she is quite successful as a communicator. Those with whom she lives and for whom she works do not share her belief in this respect, for it was her advisor who requested specialized help for her.

Here now, is a person who does not hear and has not heard for 19 years. She needs no practice in lipreading. Her language, that is, choice of words and their correct usage, presents no problem; therefore language drills are unnecessary. However, she has real difficulty in making herself intelligible to others. Her [r, l, s, z, ʒ, ʃ, tʃ, dʒ] sounds are particularly deviant. She needs work in developing more acceptable voice, for it is inadequate in loudness, quality, and inflection. Without any auditory sensitivity, speech rehabilitation becomes a complicated problem, but by substituting visual cues, progress is possible.

Case 8. Mr. Z, a well-educated man, age 65, recently had his hearing tested and was led to believe that he should be wearing a hearing aid. He accepted the idea that a hearing aid was the only solution to his problems. Careful audiological evaluation in the clinic revealed that his average level through the speech frequencies was 15 decibels for each year. His speech reception scores substantiated the pure tone results. The scores on the word discrimination task, however, were 85 per cent for the right ear and 82 per cent for the left.

Preliminary evaluation showed that he found lipreading extremely difficult. Otological reports attributed his slight loss of hearing to presbycusis (a loss which sometimes occurs as a result of the aging process).

First of all, Mr. Z must be advised against purchasing a hearing aid. It would be unwise for him to spend his money on an aid for his hearing loss is quite slight. He must be convinced that therapy in auditory training would be more advantageous. His slight loss makes it difficult for him to distinguish sounds in words which have similar acoustic characteristics. He must be helped to use the great amount of hearing which he still possesses. In addition to the auditory training, Mr. Z should be given some practice in lipreading, and a close check on his hearing should be maintained. One day Mr. Z might become a candidate for a hearing aid.

Case 9. Thirty-two-year-old Mr. A presented himself at the clinic wearing a hearing aid and requested work in lipreading. During the interview the clinician became aware that Mr. A could understand speech quite well from a distance even when the speaker's head was turned. This led, of course, to further inquiry regarding the nature of the hearing loss, its extent, and how Mr. A was handicapped by it. Answers to these questions were vague and confusing to the interviewer. Previously, Mr. A had been advised by an unskilled examiner that he sustained a severe hearing loss at certain frequencies and that he had better purchase a hearing aid. Mr. A was given a series of audiometric tests unaided. He was found to have normal hearing except at 8000 cycles per second (well above the speech-hearing range). At 8000 cycles per second his hearing threshold in both ears was at 35 decibels. It was determined later that Mr. A is the type of person who becomes unduly concerned about the slightest infirmity. When he entered the clinic he believed he was definitely handicapped and sincerely wanted help. His emotional involvement, however, had not reached proportions which indicated psychiatric referral.

Mr. A requested lipreading, but to have provided it would have been a mistake. Daily therapy was structured to demonstrate to Mr. A his ability to hear and understand speech in conditions of quiet and noise without his aid. After about one and one half months, he reluctantly but voluntarily laid his aid aside. In the following therapy sessions, attention was directed toward a slight positive nasality problem. At the end of the therapy Mr. A voluntarily admitted his mistake in purchasing the hearing aid and that at this time he does not need it.

Case 10. Bob is 17 years old and has sustained a loss of hearing since infancy. His loss involves the inner ear, and the average loss in each ear at frequencies 500-1000-2000 cycles per second is between 55 and 60 decibels. This is a moderate-to-severe handicap. Despite the fact that he has participated in auditory rehabilitation programs since early childhood, his speech is defective, but his skills in lip-reading are superior. He is objective about his handicap, and appears to possess good self and social adjustment. His binaural hearing aid lowers his speech reception threshold to 38 decibels.

Bob must concentrate upon auditory training and speech production. With his highly developed skill in lipreading, Bob receives the speech of others adequately. He needs no encouragement in accepting his handicap, and he is a well-adjusted young man. His speech, however, will stand in his way unless he improves it. Therefore, he must be given many hours of work in speech rehabilitation. With success in this area, his chances of drawing adverse attention to himself will be greatly lessened.

Case 11. Harry is a 14-year-old boy who has a perceptive loss. His loss through the speech frequencies is 20-25 decibels. Medical specialists offer no hope for reversing the loss. He has normal hearing in the low frequencies. Further, he is two grades behind in school. Fortunately, his speech has improved except for high frequency sounds (s, ʃ, θ), and generally it is quite intelligible. He has been considered dull and uninterested in his school work, but intelligence test results show him to be above average. The interviewer discovered that in three of his five classes he sits in the last seat in the row farthest from the teacher's desk. He does not reject school altogether, but he does not register real enthusiasm about any area of it except industrial arts. He is lacking in self-confidence.

Here indirect work is equally important with Harry as direct work. The principal and teachers in his school should be informed of his handicap and also of his potential. A change of attitude toward Harry by others will, in turn, help him alter his own self concept. The industrial arts teacher, of whom Harry is very fond, is the logical person to help the other teachers restructure their concepts of him. After the groundwork for readjustment has been adequately laid,

Harry can then be given direct therapy focused toward the development of lipreading skill and increased proficiency in auditory perception. Work should progress in speech rehabilitation for the purpose of making his speech more aesthetically acceptable. With normal hearing in the lower frequencies, and only a 20-25 decibel loss in the speech range, a hearing aid is not indicated.

Case 12. Mrs. B, age 78 years, was brought to the clinic by her daughter for a hearing test, possible hearing aid evaluation, and therapy. It seemed that Mrs. B did not mind her hearing deficit, and only at the urging of her daughter agreed to an audiological evaluation. Some years ago she was told by her family doctor that her hearing was not what it used to be. Audiological exam revealed a loss of 30-35 decibels in the frequencies important for hearing speech. Discrimination of the PB words was poor (78 per cent left— 76 per cent right). Her speech reception threshold in the sound field, unaided, agreed with her average pure tone loss. Several hearing aids were tested in position and found to lower Mrs. B's speech reception threshold 10-12 decibels. When asked to give a subjective evaluation of the hearing aids, in each instance she stated that the aids really "bothered me more than they helped me." Upon learning that the aids did lower her threshold for hearing, Mrs. B's daughter was insistent upon her purchasing one. The daughter seemed oblivious of her mother's desire and actual needs, but was determined to "wire" her mother so that her own lot would become easier.

Actually here is a person who might have profited from (1) an aid, (2) auditory training, and (3) lipreading practice provided she really *wanted* this kind of assistance. One should proceed cautiously, however, in exerting pressure on older people to purchase a hearing aid or to participate in a therapy program. If they wish to do so— fine. If not, then perhaps one can assume that they are happy, enjoying life, and adequately adjusting to the aging process. Perhaps this loss of hearing in old age is nature's way of protecting the organism. In the case of Mrs. B, however, the major problem is *not* in outlining rehabilitative procedures, but in providing her daughter with insights into the dynamics of the situation in which she plays an important part. Then, and only then, will Mrs. B be helped.

In these twelve cases of auditory handicaps, the long-range goals are somewhat similar, but the specific goals and needs differ greatly. In order to be most effective in management of the acoustically handicapped involving lipreading instruction, the clinician must plan his approach carefully so that it is tailored to meet the needs of those with whom he is dealing. Much valuable time may be lost and even harm done if therapy is not prepared on the basis of individual requirements.

General Suggestions for Lipreading Lesson Planning

Although it seems incompatible with the spirit of the preceding discussion to formalize rules for lipreading lesson planning, there are nevertheless some general suggestions to remember in utilizing an individualized approach.

1. Gather pertinent data that seem relevant to rehabilitation. Know the nature and degree of hearing loss, apparent self and social adjustment, relative degree of motivation, proficiency in lipreading, and so forth.

2. Plan the lessons in accordance with the data you have gathered.

3. Determine the long-range and intermediate or specific goals for each individual.

4. Construct daily lesson plans that are directed toward the intermediate or specific goals.

5. Provide an opportunity in each lesson for the handicapped person to experience success.

6. Keep the lessons interesting and challenging by employing meaningful materials.

10

EARLY LIPREADING TEXTS EMPHASIZED HOME ASSIGNMENTS consisting of mirror practice or the presentation of practice materials by a friend or member of the family. In all probability, the use of home assignments stemmed from the pedagogical background of the founders of the early lipreading systems, who assumed that any learning process must be accompanied by homework; or home assignments can be attributed to the instructor's wish to have carryover practice or to reinforce what had been learned during therapy sessions.

In present day clinical practice, little attention is paid to homework. When assignments are suggested, it may be due to the instructor's careful following of text ideas; or the instructor may believe that if no progress was made with the subject during the therapy session, then perhaps the pupil can learn by himself if provided with the proper materials. The authors feel, however, that home assignments have very little significance in

ASSIGNMENTS AND ADVICE TO PARENTS

terms of the end goals of therapy, unless they are well structured, co-ordinated with the therapy program itself, and checked and evaluated by the therapist upon completion.

In an ideal home assignment situation, mirror practice can serve two purposes. First of all, it can make the subject conscious of individual lip movement (analytical approach), and secondly, it can give an opportunity for practice with lip movements as they appear in everyday conversation. However, in reality, little practice is involved, for the individual knows ahead of time the particular phonetic or linguistic units he will be seeing, and thus he will not be motivated toward learning. A person assigned to study his own face in the mirror is an analogous example. His face seems so familiar that he does not bother to study it.

The presentation of practice materials by a family member or a friend poses problems. Not being skilled therapists, there is the danger of the mouthing of practice materials, too rapid presentation, and abnormal use of voice. Unpleasant stress is often associated with a relative telling the hard-of-hearing member of the family how to lipread. Arguments, centering around why the material cannot be understood, and statements that the hearing loss is not as bad as indicated can result. Thus it is well to avoid all assignments dealing with the presentation of linguistic and phonetic practice materials.

It is best to use home assignments that are more attitudinal; that will assist in the individual's adjustment to his hearing handicap. The cooperation of members of the family is involved, but more in the structuring of communicative and behavioral environments than in actual teaching. The use of all available communication channels should be stressed, along with efforts to provide maximum opportunities for the use of natural lipreading and auditory discrimination.

The following suggestions are offered for assignments that might be used with adults and children. These assignments will be concerned with situation or environment, not with practice of individual phonetic or linguistic units.

Adult Assignments

Adult assignments can involve three areas, (1) communication patterns, (2) self-attitudes and attitudes of others, and (3) structuring of communication environments. Through these assignments, the individual should be led to logical goals not requiring perfect or normal communication, but a measure of communication realistic for the type and degree of hearing loss. Also, the individual must be taught that communication difficulties often lie with the speaker as well as with the listener-receiver.

Communication patterns involve a delineation of possible channels of communication. The lipreader must be instructed when and how to utilize the auditory and visual channels individually, as well as when and how to utilize them together. Assignments should be structured to give the student experience with the various communication situations that he would normally encounter. Also, he should be provided with an evaluative system for a realistic appraisal of performance in the situations. For example, he may be told to converse with someone in a noisy train station, at the airport or in other circumstances where noise and confusion are present. He may be asked to converse with persons with different types of speaking voices. The extent of the assignments will depend upon the degree of hearing loss possessed by the person, as well as by the general therapy goals.

Attention must be given to the self attitudes and the attitudes of others. Assignments that require appraisals of self attitudes and the reflected attitudes of others should constitute part of the therapy. In this way the student can evaluate his own adjustment patterns.

The type of assignment to be used with the adult is based on a direct form of suggestion. The clinician suggests how the communication environment can be structured for maximum reception, and stresses that the individual himself can improve his environment. He can position himself so that he will have maximum visibility of the speaker's face; he should be aware that certain noise producing sources (telephone, radio, television, doorbell, and the like) are located in specific spots. The lipreader must realize that, in terms of interest and general conversation, language patterns are peculiar to each individual. Also, emphasis must be placed on the psychological problems attendant upon a hearing loss. In spite of difficult situations such as noisy environments or multi-speakers, it is important for the lipreader to understand that the sensory deficit will not handicap him as much as he expects. Thus, home assignments should concentrate on the individual's use of auditory discrimination and lipreading, rather than on word or sentence practice. If such a program is initiated, and faithfully carried out, the student will experience success in his communication activities.

Many teachers of lipreading suggest the use of television in home assignments. However, unless the student has two television sets, so that a normal hearing friend can listen to the audio portion of a program, then question him about what had been said, television viewing will be of little help. The lipreader must be checked, otherwise he will have no idea whether he has correctly lipread the speaker, or continued with a pattern of errors. Certain programs are more conducive to lipreading than others; news commentaries with close ups of the speaker, or programs that utilize pantomime, a good deal of movement, gesture, and close-ups are excellent. As with other assignments, the television assignment must be well thought out. All assignments must be checked by the instructor, or they will not be of much value.

It is difficult to outline specific types of assignments, for the scope and nature of the assignment depends upon the degree of hearing loss and individual attitudes. However, the assignments should be definite and realistic, in other words carefully planned so that they can be completed without great difficulty. They should be carried out at specific times or for certain lengths of time, and should be checked each day. The following descriptions of sample assignments will serve to clarify the suggestions presented in the discussion of assignments for the hard of hearing adult.

1. A 52-year-old male with a hearing loss restricted to the higher frequencies (2000, 4000, and 8000 cycles per second). The major problem centered around the joint use of audition and vision. The following types of assignments were used.

    a. A close evaluation of communication situations that are encountered each day. List difficult and easy situations.

    b. Analysis of difficult situations in terms of speaker, environmental noise, and structure of the communication situation.

    c. Analysis of speakers who are difficult and easy to hear.

    d. Evaluation of degree of hearing and lipreading used in each situation.

    e. Self structuring of specific communication situations; committee meetings, student conferences, classroom lectures, and social conversations.

   f. Application of combined use of hearing and lipreading. Start with ten minute practice periods. Pick out one person and see how well you can understand him. Extend observation time. Increase number of persons observed.

2. A 22-year-old senior majoring in pharmacy was referred to the clinic by the dean of his college. This young man exhibited good auditory discrimination with a slight-to-moderate, flat type of hearing loss. However, he made little use of visual cues, as was indicated by the results of initial testing and observation.

   a. Tachistoscopic practice at exposure speed of 1/25th of a second. Start with five digits and work up through seven digits.

   b. View Mason Visual Hearing films. Films 1 through 10. Turn in answer sheets after each film.

   c. Describe ten people you have met. Describe their facial features.

   d. Describe the instructor who is the easiest to lipread. Describe the instructor who is the most difficult to lipread. Analyze their speaking habits.

   e. Concentrate on trying to lipread at least three persons a day. Concentrate on one person in each of your classes.

   f. Study difficulties you have experienced in various communication situations.

   g. Visit the bowling alley in the Union building. Describe what success you experience while conversing with a friend in this situation.

3. A 19-year-old girl enrolled in nurse's training. A slight-to-moderate hearing loss in the lower frequencies and a severe loss in the higher frequencies. This girl did not make adequate use of auditory or visual cues.

   a. Make a point of proper seating in class rooms. Try positions in the front and on either side of the class room.

   b. Evaluation of social situations. What situations are avoided? What people create special problems? What are the problems?

   c. Participate in at least three social situations each day.

   d. Listen to one radio program a day. See how much you can recall.

   e. View the Mason films and the ten films in the first Morkovin film series. Turn in completed answer sheets.

   f. Carry out weekly assignments with therapist. Therapist will ask questions keyed to planned conversation situations. The therapist will suggest methods of structuring each situation. Suggestions will be offered on how the client can make use of information about the general nature of the situation.

Two other types of assignments can be used with adults. The first involves directed reading, and has value for the highly motivated, intelligent client who wishes more information on the nature of his hearing loss, the problems encountered by the acoustically handicapped, and the types of rehabilitation aids that will be of benefit. Articles from the *Hearing News* or materials prepared by the American Hearing Society, and such books as the Canfield and Davis texts listed at the end of this chapter can be used. It is imperative that the readings be discussed and all questions answered.

The second involves situational practice in terms of assignments. A therapist accompanies the student and selects practice situations, suggesting what the client should be doing in terms of his use of auditory and visual cues. After each assignment is finished, the student and therapist discuss how the assignment was handled, the correct procedures used, and methods of improving reception in these situations.

Children's Assignments

Assignments for children can involve the participation of the parents or participation of the child alone. As with adults, the assignments should be specific and geared to the capabilities of the child. They should be worked in with the general therapy plan. Usually the home assignment is employed only if the co-operation of the parents can be obtained. If assignments are to be used, they should involve "good listening," and be specific as to time and place. The child must be ready to perform such assignments. In other words, he must understand their purpose and have sufficient objectivity to carry them out. The major emphasis for the parents should be placed on the proper structuring of the communication situation. Thus, if the parents are to talk to the child, they should make sure that they have his attention and have positioned themselves so that he can hear and see them. There must be no calling from one room to the next, or the issuing of orders and suggestions when the child can-not see the parent. Also, parents should not be upset if the child asks for repetitions or does not receive the message correctly the first time. Home assignments for children should be a family affair, and be so organized that they occur at the same time every day or week. In this way, all members of the family are alerted to the problems of communication. The assignment should deal with general story telling, or conversation practice.

It might be well to arrange the assignments so that the child must correct or change the communication patterns of his parents. If the home assignment involves an activity, such as a visit to the zoo or a day at the ball game, the lesson should be structured so that the parents can report the events. They should also receive advice on how they can structure situations so that the child receives the neces-sary communication experience. The parents must realize that their child's hearing handicap is not as bad as they think. They should be told to observe their children's normalities rather than his abnormal-ities. Unless the parents have been thoroughly coached or have observed a trained therapist, they should not be allowed to present word or sentence practice materials to the child.

Two examples of assignments are offered. One demonstrates a direct assignment for a child, the other a parental assignment.

An eight-year-old girl enrolled in the third grade was referred to the clinic by a school nurse who reported that the child was having difficulty hearing her teachers. This girl was an intelligent youngster who had a reported score on the Stanford-Binet of 138. The first as-signment involved an analysis of the type of materials that provided the greatest difficulties for her in the listening situation. Other assign-ments dealt with an analysis of what parts of speech gave her trouble, what parts of sentences were missed, what teachers posed problems; an analysis of her parent's communication habits, and a final analysis of difficulties in listening to television, and difficulties encountered during play. In essence, this was practice in guided listening. As this young girl carried out the assignments listed above, she began to make extensive use of both auditory and visual cues. A discussion of the results of the assignments provided the therapist with an op-portunity to suggest methods of improving speech reception in each of the situations, as well as to describe the problem areas that re-quired closer attention and prior structuring.

As an example of parental assignments, the case of a five-year-old boy with a moderate- to severe-hearing loss will be used. The parents of this youngster were "busy" people. The father held an executive position in a large insurance firm, and the mother was an active club woman. There were two other children in the family, both girls, older than the boy under discussion. One of the first problems the parents had to meet was to provide time for communication with their hard of hearing son. This involved setting aside a certain period each evening for guided communication. The therapist stressed their need to be patient, and to make sure their son was getting what they said. It was impressed upon them that all members of the family should direct communication toward the boy. Also, they were to revise the impressions that they had left with their friends and neighbors regarding their son. It was suggested that the neighbors should be told that they could talk to the boy and that he could hear what they said. The parents were loaned an auditory training unit, were instructed in its use, and guided in the type of settings to be employed. Appropriate practice materials, recorded as well as printed, were provided. Demonstrations of the use of the microphone, and methods of combining visual and auditory cues were given. The use of the auditory training unit was preparatory to the wearing of a hearing aid. Initially, the parents resisted the fitting of an aid, but guided practice with the auditory training unit led them to the acceptance of the continuous use of amplified sound. Stress was placed upon the need to give their son information about things that occurred around him, on vacation trips and week-ends. The parents were made to realize that he needed as much information as any youngster his age. They were told to assemble a working vocabulary of frequently used words and phrases, and verbalize for the child what he was doing. It was further suggested that they illustrate their discussions through the use of objects or pictures. Thus, the parents were guided to provide proper listening environments, proper presentation of information, and to accept the idea of his wearing a hearing aid. They also came to realize that their son had many positive skills and required as much love and attention as his sisters.

Advice to Parents

The basic information, that children must utilize certain communication channels, should be conveyed to parents. In the case of the aurally handicapped child, these channels include the visual and auditory modalities. The child must be ready to utilize any or all of these channels. Parents should structure the situation before they start conversing with the child. Also, they should remember their goals, or what they hope to accomplish, when they speak to him. If they want him to react, they must be certain that he has received the correct stimulus. The parents will need a great deal of patience. They should be trained to observe the behavior of their child so that they can correctly evaluate his response to verbal stimuli. They must not let the child obtain things by not hearing, or by not apparently hearing. The child should be required to participate in the communication act before he receives a reward or recognition.

Another major problem is that of behavior dynamics. Many times parents cannot decide if the child's behavior is a function of the handicap, or symbolic of something else. The parents should be informed that the child with a hearing loss still has all of the normal behavior patterns of a nonhandicapped child. In no instance should the handicap become the focus of parental thinking; it is far better for them to assume that they have a normal child with a handicap.

The distinction between a deaf and a hard of hearing child must be emphasized. Parents should realize that the hard of hearing child is not going to have the problems of the deaf child. This can be effectively presented by detailing the problems of the deaf child— the lag in language development, the lack of abstracting ability, the lack of environmental input. Parents can gain a great deal of information about their hard of hearing child through assigned readings. Such reading will also serve as a framework for discussion. A few of the books that might be suggested are listed at the end of this chapter.

Parents can also make use of the materials provided by the American Hearing Society. However, it is important that these materials be discussed with the parents. The therapist should point out that certain statements, only, apply to their children, while other statements have no relevance.

If the child is wearing a hearing aid, the therapist can provide considerable information as to its use, the problems that will be encountered, and the type of approach the parents can use. In this instance the little book by Ronnei and Porter[1] may be of some help.

---

[1] Eleanor C. Ronnei and J. Porter, *Tim and His Hearing Aid* (New York: Dodd, Mead & Company, 1952).

This cartoon account of the wearing of a hearing aid will be useful for parents to communicate information to their child. The care of a hearing aid is important. Parents should know about tone settings, changing of batteries, and the problems children can encounter while wearing a hearing aid. During the initial use of a hearing aid a schedule should be followed, for a child must be worked gradually toward the full time wearing of the aid.

Information can also be presented through Parent Teacher Association meetings or through meetings of special problems groups. The therapist can utilize motion pictures as well as illustrated lectures dealing with the anatomy of the ear, the wearing of a hearing aid, causes of hearing losses, and rehabilitative procedures. He can answer questions about specific problems. The therapist who follows the listing of films and educational materials that appear in the *Journal of Speech and Hearing Disorders, ASHA, Volta Review, Hearing News,* and *Exceptional Children* should not want for such materials.

The trained therapist will be able to offer a great deal of assistance to parents. This assistance may be worth many hours of direct therapy with the aurally handicapped child. The parents need to have an understanding of the nature of the defect, the personality patterns of their child, and the ways in which they can help their child. The therapist can provide this material in a direct manner through lectures and conferences, or in an indirect manner through guided readings.

Parental Group Conference

Parental group conferences afford the therapist an excellent opportunity to present information, answer questions, and lead group discussion. Such group situations are rewarding if a catalytic type of parent is included in the group. Answers to questions usually have relevance for parents other than those asking the question. Such parental sessions can best operate in an informal structure. The authors led group meetings with satisfactory results. The sessions described below covered a ten week period and involved five to eight parents. In most instances, only mothers attended the meetings. Fathers were encouraged to attend, but because of employment and baby sitting duties some of the fathers could not come. There was one meeting a week which lasted for about an hour.

FIGURE 15. *Parental group session. Information is being presented relative to the nature of various types of hearing loss. (Courtesy American Hearing Society.)*

The following topics were included in the ten week series of discussions:

1. Anatomy of the ear. Models, charts, and discussions including types of pathologies and types of loss exhibited by the children.

2. Examination for hearing loss. Demonstration of the audiometer and types of hearing tests. Discussion of what the otologist does and what the audiologist does.

3. Rehabilitation procedures—medical and educational.

4. Lipreading and auditory training. Demonstration of each type of procedure. Suggestions on how the approaches can be used in the home.

5. Home structuring. Role of parents and other members of the family in improving the communication skills of the child.

6. Effects of a hearing loss upon speech. Discussion of speech conservation and speech problems exhibited by the children.

7. Personality patterns associated with hearing loss. Discussion of development of personality and communication patterns.

8. The hearing aid. Description and demonstration. Discussion of types of hearing aids worn by the children.

9. Discussion of child development and the effects of hearing loss upon such development. Discussion of early developmental history of their own children.

10. Individual conferences. Discussion of child's progress and future planning.

Assignments for parents can involve passive or active participation. The viewing of films and the reading of assigned materials constitute a passive form of participation. The discussion occurring in the group situation and in structured interview situations involves active participation.

Assignments have their place in a therapy program, but only if they are organized and meaningful. Most of the assignments should be of an indirect nature with no direct practice with linguistic or phonetic materials. The nature of the assignments depend upon the type and degree of defect, as well as upon the personality of the child and the parents. If the therapist has to strive mightily to develop an assignment, it is best to forget it.

MATERIALS FOR READING ASSIGNMENTS

1. Canfield, Norton, *Hearing: A Handbook for Laymen,* New York: Doubleday & Company, Inc., 1959.

2. Davis, H., *Hearing and Deafness,* New York: Rinehart & Company, Inc., 1947.

3. Hoverstein, G. and J. Keaster, *Suggestions to the Parents of a Hard of Hearing Child,* American Academy of Opthalmology and Otolaryngology, 1959.

4. *If You Have a Deaf Child,* Urbana, Illinois: University of Illinois Press, 1949.

5. Myklebust, H. R., *Your Deaf Child: A Guide for Parents,* Springfield, Illinois: C. C. Thomas, 1950.

ADDRESSES

1. The American Hearing Society, 919 18th Street, N.W., Washington 6, D.C. This agency publishes the *Hearing News.*

2. The Volta Bureau, 1537 35th Street, N.W., Washington, D.C. This agency publishes *The Volta Review.*

3. American Speech and Hearing Association, 1001 Connecticut

Avenue, N.W., Washington 6, D.C. This agency publishes the *Journal of Speech and Hearing Disorders* and *ASHA*.

4. The Council for Exceptional Children, 1201 Sixteenth Street, N.W., Washington 6, D.C. This agency publishes the journal *Exceptional Children*.

II

WITH THE DEVELOPMENT OF THE CONCEPT OF EDUCA-
tional television and the attendant increase in television
facilities, the interest of lipreading instructors has been
aroused to the possibilities of the use of such equipment
in the teaching of lipreading. In one way television
solves the problem of "no voice versus voice" in the
presentation of lipreading materials. If the instructor
wishes to utilize voice for part of the lesson, he requests
that the auditory circuit be left on or the volume turned
down to desired levels. Also, no voice (in the sense of
turning off the sound) can be used without exaggeration or slowed up delivery. Such lipreading lessons can
be administered over the facilities of commercial or
educational stations, or closed circuit systems. In this
latter instance, the lessons can be given in a school or
clinical environment without the problem of schedul-
ing viewing time.

Too few agencies have made use of television in the

TELEVISION AND LIPREADING INSTRUCTION

teaching of lipreading. The first published account of its use in this area appeared in 1955. The article describes a series of 12 programs presented over the facilities of Station KTHE in conjunction with the University of Southern California and the Hearing Center of Metropolitan Los Angeles. Moore,[1] in her description of the program, states that its primary purpose was to change attitudes of the public toward the deaf and hard of hearing as well as to promote understanding of the problems of these handicapped groups. The program utilized the Morkovin Life Situation Motion Pictures and skits depicting everyday speech situations. The scripts were written by Dr. Boris Morkovin who also served as moderator of the program. In 1956 the University of Nebraska sponsored a series of 16 lessons. The series used a manual that could be purchased by viewers. The program, as described by Cypresasen and McBride,[2] was directed toward definite instruction in lipreading with emphasis on a phonetic approach. Syllable practice, word practice in conversational phrases, common sayings, and questions and answers were used as part of the training program. Several novel approaches were employed. First of all, materials were presented on a revolving drum so that a visual check of the instructional materials could be made by the students. Also, a practice group (two students) was used to provide live "feedback." The image of the students was superimposed along with the image of the instructor so that the give and take of a classroom situation or therapy situation was shown. In 1958, Crawley[3] reported on a lipreading series presented in conjunction with the University of Wisconsin television station. Twenty minutes of each of 20 half-hour programs were devoted to lipreading practice. The remainder of the time was spent in presenting material relative to the social and medical aspects of a hearing loss. The programs were kinescoped and were viewed by an experimental group of 50 subjects who were to be tested to ascertain any gains made in lipreading ability because of exposure to the program. The lipreading materials consisted of words and sentences utilized in a synthetic approach. No one method of teaching lipreading was used; it was, rather, an eclectic approach. The Denver Hearing Society also sponsored a lipreading program over the facilities of station KRMA-

[1] Lucelia Moore, "Television as a Medium for Teaching Speechreading and Speech," *The Volta Review*, 57 (1955), pp. 263-264.

[2] Lucile Cypresasen and Jack McBride, "Lipreading Lessons On Television," *The Volta Review*, 58 (1956), pp. 346-348.

[3] Edward F. Crawley, "Television and the Hearing Handicapped," *Hearing News*, 26, No. 1 (January 1958), pp. 3-4.

TV in Denver. The program, as described by Kaho,[4] consisted of a 26-week series of lipreading lessons. Kaho stated in the article, "It is amazing how clearly these (lip) movements show up when the TV camera is focused on the mouth of the teacher and the entire television screen shows just the lip, tongue and teeth action." The lessons were built around situational practice, and were divided into three sections; an initial section which was devoted to an interview with a guest, a second part devoted to the teaching of new sounds, and a third section which dealt with situational lipreading practice. The program was a success in terms of presenting lipreading instruction to a large number of people. Also, it served as an excellent means of informing the public about the problems of the aurally handicapped. In 1959, O'Neill[5] reported on a television series produced at Ohio State University. A major portion of the article is reproduced here for the purpose of presenting a detailed example of a planned series of lipreading instruction.

The series involved eight weekly programs. Each program was half an hour in length. The individual programs were divided into two time segments. The first segment, ten minutes in length, was devoted to demonstrations, lectures and discussions with guest "experts." The second segment was 18 minutes in length and involved the actual presentation of a lipreading lesson. The lessons utilized a modified Nitchie method and involved presentation of key words and accompanying sentences. The key words were presented audibly and visually. The visual presentation was accomplished through the use of a large chart which displayed the key words used in the lesson. The words were presented individually for recognition practice and in groups for contrast practice. After this short drill the sentences were given. Before each group of four sentences was delivered, the key word which appeared in the sentences was presented with both visual and auditory re-enforcement. Before each of the four sentences was given, a voiced statement pertaining to the thought of the sentence was presented. For example the sentence, "I would like to have your view on the subject," was preceded by the statement, "This sentence is about something a wife may never say to her husband." Immediately after the sentence was presented *without* voice it was delivered again with voice. So that the

---

[4] Elizabeth E. Kaho, "This Is Lipreading on TV," *Hearing News*, 26, No. 3 (May 1958), pp. 7-8 and 18.

[5] John O'Neill, "A Televised Lipreading Series," *Central States Speech Journal*, 10 (Winter 1959), pp. 35-37.

viewers could check the accuracy of their responses, the sentence was then offered on an Executive Type Teleprompter. Approximately 12 key words and 48 sentences were given during each program. At the end of this formal section of the lesson, a group of ten common expressions was presented. These expressions were taken from the Ordman and Ralli manual.[6] The viewers were alerted to this section by a caption on the Teleprompter and a verbal statement from the instructor. Each program ended with the presentation of a riddle or a short saying which was revealed at the beginning of the next program. The last minutes were devoted to a rapid summary of the program as well as a short description of the forthcoming one.

The individual lessons involved a different sound for each program. The lessons proceeded from a visible consonant sound to a somewhat obscured consonant sound (*p*, *b* and *m* through *w* and *wh* sounds).

A medium-sized set was utilized for the series. The back walls of the set consisted of brightly painted pegboard arranged in a series of staggered patterns. On part of the back wall were two blackboards as well as a large space for the presentation of visual aids. The set was divided into two areas. One of the areas contained easy chairs, several low tables, and a blackboard. This area was used during the first part of the program. The second part of the set contained a waist high lectern which also housed the small teleprompter. Also included was a blackboard and an easel for the presentation of visual aids. Two cameras were used during the program. One camera was used for long as well as "tight" shots during the introductory phase of the program. During the lesson proper, the two cameras were utilized for selected close-up shots. A boom microphone was used for audio pickup. Also, on several occasions one of the cameras was used for slide projection pickup.

The order and content of each program was as follows:

1st Program: Discussion of purposes of the program and description of the nature of lipreading. Administration of short lipreading test. Introductory lesson using salutations and materials dealing with foods, cars, and days of the week.

2nd Program: Discussion of anatomy of the ear, pathologies of the ear, and role of medical therapy. Lesson on *p*, *b*, and *m* sounds. Section on "What People Say—About the Weather."

[6] Kathryn Ordman and Mary P. Ralli, *What People Say* (New York: The Nitchie School of Lipreading, 1949).

3rd Program: Discussion of methods of testing hearing—pure tone and speech reception tests as well as a discussion of the testing of the hearing of pre-school children. Lesson on *f* and *v* sounds. Section on "What People Say—At the Dinner Table."

4th Program: Discussion of lipreading training through the use of silent motion picture films. Showing of two lipreading films produced by Marie Mason. Lesson on *s* and *z* sound.

5th Program: Discussion of value of auditory training. Demonstration of use of residual hearing. Lesson on *sh* and *ch* sounds. Section on "What People Say—At Election Time."

6th Program: Discussion of the value of visual training in the development of skill in lipreading. Demonstration of tachistoscopic and flash-card training. Lesson on *t* and *d* sounds. Section on "What People Say—At the Movies."

7th Program: Discussion of Hearing Aids—their fitting and principles of correct usage. Lesson on *w* and *wh* sounds. Section on "What People Say—About Hearing Aids."

8th Program: Discussion of mental hygiene for the hard of hearing and the value of speech conservation. Readministration of initial lipreading test. Listeners were asked to evaluate their progress. Section on "What People Say—Upon Leaving."

One of the basic problems encountered with such a television program is the lack of response from a live therapy group. In order to compensate for this lack of response the lesson was previewed with an adult therapy group the day before the program was scheduled. In this way, the sections that proved to be most difficult were anticipated. Consequently, when presented on television, it was possible to role play the therapy session in terms of repetitions of materials, amplifications of materials, and so on.

Larr and Hempen[7] described the use of closed circuit television in the teaching of lipreading. In this particular study a teacher presented speech reading materials in a closed circuit television studio. Students viewed the image of the teacher on a monitor screen in another studio. The results of pre and post tests indicated that students made noticeable improvement during five class meetings. Also, it was found that head and neck images and upper torso images were lipread more successfully than head only, or lips only images. A 45-degree angle of presentation of the face was slightly superior to a

[7] Alfred L. Larr and C. Hempen, "Speech Reading Through Closed Circuit Television," a paper presented at the 34th Annual Convention of the American Speech and Hearing Association (New York, November 19th, 1958).

front view. According to the authors, the use of closed circuit tele-vision is a highly motivating teaching device.

Possible Values of Television

The use of television in the instruction of lipreading is a new con-cept, and at the present time the hearing therapist is trying to justify its use. A basic problem is one of ascertaining how many people can benefit from lipreading training when it is presented on a mass communication basis. Needless to say; on a national basis there is no market for such training, but within restricted regional areas, it may have some value. A large scale research study must be under-taken to see if there is a demand for such a series. It has already been shown that the mechanics of television can be successfully adapted for the teaching of lipreading. One immediate educational benefit offered by television training is an excellent teaching environment. Well organized lessons can be provided with extensive use of teach-ing aids. Also, it is possible to provide clinical assistance to individ-uals who cannot be reached through the medium of speech and hearing clinics or traveling therapists. Thus, lipreading training would become more readily available. However, a major problem for the television therapist is the lack of contact with the client. Learning does not proceed as well when a therapist is not in direct contact with the individual students. In a face to face situation, ef-forts of the therapist can be directed toward the individual needs of the student. Also, instructor efficiency may drop without any "re-sponse" from his students. It might be better to look at the benefits of television without bothering with the problem of the servicing of scattered areas or a large audience. It is more important to analyze how the use of television can lead to better instruction. The prob-lem is not how many lipreaders can be reached, but rather how many individuals can be taught to lipread. In this context, it is well to view the advantages of television, closed circuit as well as educa-tional and commercial television.

One of the major advantages of television therapy lies in varying the image the subject is viewing. In other words, the viewer can see a close-up of lips, the face, upper torso, or full body length, and at-tention is directed to particular aspects of the lipreading act. Thus, individual training can be administered in terms of specific viewing angles, and visual attention can be directed for the viewer much more effectively than in the routine lipreading therapy situation. With the use of the audio circuit it is possible to present lessons with or without sound, or with reduced sound. In this way, the instructor can avoid the use of no voice, whispered speech, or a viewing window. Also, it is possible to use visual props with the subject's attention focused directly on them. With no direct contact between the instructor and the viewer, some of the pressure may be removed from the student lipreader.

If a closed circuit system is used with the instructor stationed in an adjacent room with a one way mirror, he can have contact with the cases. With a television setup, the instructor has a fixed therapy area; thus he is aware, ahead of time, of the space he will be able to use. Also, if the instructor has a monitor screen in front of him, he can observe his manner of presentation, in other words, he will have feedback of what he is doing and how he appears. Thus he has a much more accurate knowledge of his manner of presentation.

Charts can be prepared and used to full advantage because of visual close-up. Also, through the use of a memory drum device, or a teleprompter, it is possible for the individual case to be aware of the material being presented.

The major worth of commercial television is that it can inform others of the problems of the aurally handicapped. It can provide information on how the aurally handicapped are helped, the complications of learning to lipread, and what can be done to assist in the teaching of lipreading. With commercial sponsorship it is possible to film the sessions via kinescope or magnetic tape and therefore make the lessons available for others elsewhere.

The use of closed circuit television tends to restrict the size of the viewing audience since the monitor screens for such systems are not too large. It is true that commercial or educational television stations are able to reach older individuals or shut-ins, who cannot make a trip to a clinic, or those living in an area not serviced by a hearing clinic. But, exactly how many persons would take advantage of such service? How would the listeners know what mistakes they are making? Who would check on their progress and who would arrange for the therapy regimen? Merely exposing a person to lipreading is not going to make a lipreader out of him.

In light of these possible difficulties, the following suggestions are offered for, (a) a series on an educational or commercial station, and (b) a closed-circuit television system. The primary purpose of such programs could be the selecting of individuals who could benefit most from lipreading training, and determining whether those individuals would be interested enough to continue in a conventional type of therapy program. With these two points in mind, the types of programs that might be offered are briefly described.

Possible Use of Television

Educational or Commercial Television

One of the major problems occurring with such forms of television is the arrangement of suitable viewing times. In fact, determining an ideal viewing time for a television program devoted to lipreading poses a difficult problem. With commercial stations, it is difficult to obtain viewing times during the afternoon or during the prize evening hours. Also, it would be foolish to be in competition with any of the popular network or local programs. An early evening or mid-afternoon hour would seem to be the best viewing time since other members of the family might be available to assist the student lipreader. The program format would have to follow a general, informal pattern. The lessons would have to be structured to stress a synthetic approach to lipreading. This means that individual lessons would be built around words or sentences, rather than around a single sound as in the typical analytical approach. Also, a manual should be prepared for use with such a program.

The viewer should be continually aware of what occurs on the program. Thus, the instructor must use repetition, visual aids, and the auditory channel. Also, all bodily movements should be relatively slow and smooth and the instructor should keep his face to his audience at all times. In planning programs, it is necessary to pre-plan the sequence of shots so that the director will know exactly what type of shot is required, either close-up or distance shot of the instructor or visual aids. One important factor, not to be overlooked, is the type of background used in the set. A background with many symmetrical designs will be confusing and distracting to the lipreader. As for the lesson itself, it is well to use a lead-in pattern presenting visual and auditory cues so that the viewers have some idea of what is happening. It might be well to utilize a voice and no voice approach. The coverage of materials, sounds, or topics must be limited. The lesson cannot cover too much and repetition will be necessary. The lipreading lesson materials should be of a familiar nature, dealing with current items of interest. The general presentation of the lessons can follow the procedure suggested in the previously mentioned O'Neill article.

Closed-Circuit Television

A closed-circuit system will involve, at a minimum, the following pieces of equipment: a camera, lens system, a monitor system, and connecting cables. The minimum cost of such a system would be approximately $1,800. More elaborate systems can be assembled. These can include several cameras, several monitor screens, a switching system, remote control equipment, and a series of close-up lenses. A maximum cost for such a complete system would be around $30,000. The following establishments provide closed-circuit equipment:

> Blonder-Tongue Laboratories, Inc., 9 Alling Street, Newark 2, New Jersey
>
> Dage Electronics Division, Thompson Products Inc., Michigan City, Indiana.
>
> Diamond Television, Lancaster, Ohio.
>
> Kintel Division of Cohu Electronics, Inc., 5725 Kearny Villa Road, San Diego 11, California.
>
> Radio Corporation of America, Camden, New Jersey.
>
> Dumont Corporation, Allen B. DuMont Labs., Inc., Clifton, N.J.

The closed-circuit method of presentation has greater flexibility than the educational or commercial systems. An ideal approach involves at least one camera and one monitor screen. The instructor can be in an adjacent room observing through a viewing port, or he can be in the same room as the viewers. The viewers would be watching the monitor screen which presents close-up shots of the speaker's face or lips. Such a system requires at least two persons, one to operate the camera and manipulate the lenses for close-up shots, and the other to present the lesson materials; or the camera can be left on the same setting, then only one instructor is required. More elaborate systems include several cameras, several monitor screens, and a remote control system. With this arrangement, the instructor monitors his own performance and selects several camera angles to be used. The closed circuit will allow the instructor a great deal of flexibility, for he can talk directly to the viewers and adapt his presentation to the difficulties experienced by individual members of the class. Manner of lesson procedure, in this instance, can follow conventional therapy approaches.

Characteristics of the Instructor

The instructor must operate as if he were talking to one individual. In fact, he should use an approach similar to the one he would use in conducting a therapy session with a single individual. As a result, teaching via television becomes intimate and the instructor needs a warm, understanding personality. Stiffness and monotony must be avoided. A great deal is required of the therapist. He must be able to anticipate points of confusion. This can come only after extensive experience with lipreading cases and clinical activities. It might be well for the therapist to test most of his lessons on a live therapy group in order to anticipate problem areas as well as to try out his technique.

One final point. Educational and commercial television stations require the instructor to place himself in the hands of the station staff. He can give his ideas, but then he must adjust them to conform to the limitations of space, equipment, and the idiosyncrasies of the director and his staff.

A Pilot Program

One of the authors has recently completed teaching a college course in the theories of lipreading. The laboratory portion of the course, which comprised two of the five hours the class met each week, was devoted to the presentation of televised lipreading lessons. Lessons, constructed and presented by the students, were centered around many different themes. The only requirements were that there be a central theme, observation of the 20 minute time allotment for the lessons, and that the viewers be provided with answer sheets. During each lesson the viewers wrote responses on their specially prepared answer sheets. At the end of the hour the answer sheets were collected and graded. Grades were posted conspicuously on a chart and seemed to provide a good source of motivation. Analysis of scores, obtained by pretraining and post-training testing with a recently developed filmed test of lipreading, reveals that the class as a whole made significant improvement in lipreading performance as a result of training.

It is evident that lipreading instruction can be presented through television. Lipreading instruction encompasses the type of subject material and manner of presentation that adapts well to television. Teachers of lipreading need to undertake extensive research to discover those aspects of television that will improve lipreading instruction. If television is approached in this fashion, rather than in the manner of just using it as a novelty, it will become vital in the teaching of lipreading.

APPENDIX A

VISUAL HEARING TESTS FOR CHILDREN

Two simple tests* were constructed to be used experimentally in this study. Test I, Form A, and its alternate, Form B, were designed to determine a young pre-school deaf child's ability to recognize the visible kinesthetic speech pattern set up when five simple test words are spoken individually, and to translate these visible movements into verbal concepts. Test II, Form A and Form B, included ten words of increasing visible and experiential difficulty intended to measure achievement of a slightly higher level. Nouns were used in both tests. They are here listed:

Test I
Form A: fish, ball, top, cow, flower
Form B: baby, cat, car, shoe, cup

Test II
Form A: woman, boat, fork, man, comb, dog, table, boy, chair, girl
Form B: sheep, cap, book, knife, glove, spoon, muff, glass, coat, horse

A test film was constructed to present the test content. Both tests were on 16mm motion-picture film and the cinematographic technique was the same for both Tests I and II. The following three steps were utilized in the films.

The Cinematographic Technique

First Step. A motion picture scene is shown in which a speaker and two deaf children are seated at a table, on which may be seen concrete objects illustrating the five test nouns. Holding up each object in turn, the speaker pronounces its name, turning successively in profile as she speaks to the child on either side, and finally speaks a third time directly into the camera.

Second Step. (1) The speaker, without indicating the object, speaks each of the five nouns in altered serial order; the children in the picture respond by holding up each object as it is spoken. (2) A pictorial chart, a facsimile of the test blanks used in the test proper (in the succeeding step), is then shown. The pictured children are seen making a large cross on the picture representing the spoken word called for by the speaker.

Third step. This is the test proper. The speaker appearing alone gives

* Mason Multiple Choice Tests for Children, devised by Marie K. Mason, Speech and Hearing Clinic, Ohio State University.

the same five nouns in varied order, speaking directly into the camera. This gives the effect of addressing herself personally to the children being tested. Each spoken word is preceded by a number which corresponds to the numbered row of pictures on the test blank and which contains the illustrated test word. The testees' response is a large cross drawn on the picture which for them objectifies the words pronounced by the speaker.

Key

Ohio State University
Columbus, Ohio

Marie K. Mason,
Speech & Hearing Clinic

VISUAL HEARING TEST

Name _____ School _____
       last   first

Age _____ Male_____Fem._____ Grade _____

Date_____ 19_____ City _____ State _____

Test Number I - Form A

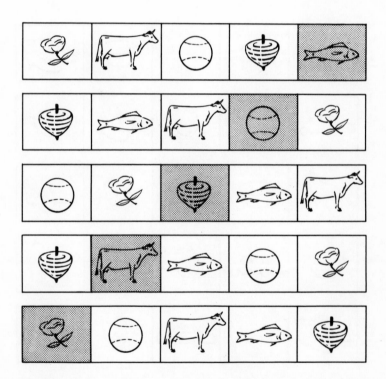

In each row of pictures the child will draw a cross (X) which illustrates the
Visual Hearing test word.

VISUAL HEARING TEST I—FORM A

Key

Ohio State University   Marie K. Mason,
Columbus, Ohio   Speech & Hearing Clinic

VISUAL HEARING TEST

Name _____ School _____
          last   first
Age _____ Male _____ Fem. _____ Grade _____

Date _____ 19 _____ City _____ State _____

Test Number I - Form B

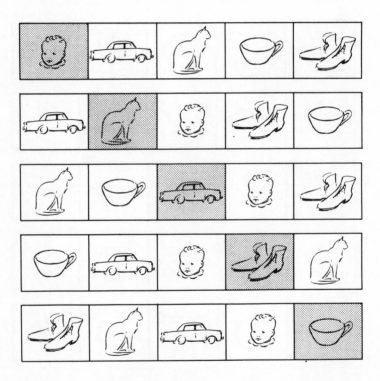

In each row of pictures the child will draw a cross (X) which illustrates the
Visual Hearing test word.

VISUAL HEARING TEST I—FORM B

VISUAL HEARING TEST II—FORM B

APPENDIX B

VISUAL HEARING FILMS

*A Complete Sequence of Instructional Units
for Use in Teaching
Visual Comprehension of Speech*

by

Marie K. Mason

VISUAL HEARING IS THE COMPREHENSION OF SPOKEN THOUGHT THROUGH THE interpretation of visual stimuli when response to auditory stimuli is inadequate or entirely lacking. A two-fold process, visual hearing is phonetic in its translation of visible movements into vowels and consonants and mental, or cognitive, in its transformation of the speaker's visible speech patterns into meaningful thought patterns.

The course of instruction in visual hearing described in the following pages is based upon a series of thirty 16-mm. silent color films, each running approximately eight minutes, in which various speakers are presented reading script material. Each film is a complete instructional unit, and the thirty films are arranged in a sequence proceeding from the easier to the more difficult aspects of visual hearing. Film I introduces the student to some of the basic principles underlying the visual comprehension of speech. Each succeeding film introduces a new phonetic element or principle, all of the English consonants being considered in their initial, medial, and final positions in words and in the combinations characteristic of normal speech. The Standard American diphthongs are presented in Film VI, but no film is reserved exclusively for treatment of the vowels. Films V, X, XX, and XXX are devoted to a review of the visible clues characteristic of the phonetic elements presented in preceding films.

Each film assignment comprises three parts. The first part, which serves as a text, announces the assignment topic and displays several title cards bearing printed sentences to be read by the student previous to their utterance by the speaker; the second part shows the speaker voicing the remainder of the script with no printed clues to assist the student in his visual interpretation of the speaker's words; the third part contains questions which the student may be expected to answer from his analysis of the speaker's visible speech manifestations. In a majority of the films the script material employed consists of unrelated sentences to develop alertness in making visual discriminations; and to provide a background of visual memory of spoken sounds, each sentence contains a specific consonant frequently repeated. To develop the student's ability to synthesize, certain film scripts contain also a series of related sentences, and several films are devoted to the connected discussion of a single topic.

DESCRIPTION OF THE FILMS

Film Number	Phonetic Content	Script Content	Objectives
I (Female Speaker)	Introduction to the visual comprehension of speech.	Familiar greetings, questions, and comments used in daily conversation.	To develop confidence through the successful visual translation of simple spoken language.
II (Female Speaker)	Group I of bi-labial consonants: [ʍ] as in *"where"* [w] as in *"wear"*	Series of paired sentences, one sentence of each pair containing the consonant [ʍ], the other containing [w].	To provide opportunity for study and analysis of the visible characteristics of the consonants [ʍ] and [w] in combination with various vowel sounds.
III (Female Speaker)	Group II of bi-labial consonants: [p] as in *"pie"* [b] as in *"buy"* [m] as in *"my"*	Groups of three sentences, one sentence in each group repeating frequently one or more of the three consonants.	To teach visual analysis and recognition of the consonants [p], [b], and [m] and the visible clues which differentiate them from [ʍ] and [w].
IV (Female Speaker)	The labio-dental consonants: [f] as in *"fail"* [v] as in *"vale"*	Unrelated sentences in which [f] and [v] occur frequently.	To identify the visible characteristics of the consonants [f] and [v].
V (Male Speaker)	Review of the phonetic elements presented in Films I, II, III, IV.	A speaker enumerates various kinds of merchandise to be found in a five and ten cent store.	To develop visual memory span and the ability to synthesize through the recognition of longer thought units in connected speech.
VI (Female Speaker)	The diphthongs: [aɪ] as in *"ice"* [ou] as in *"go"* [ɔɪ] as in *"boy"* [ɪu] as in *"few"* [au] as in *"how"* [eɪ] as in *"ate"*	Groups of paired sentences, each pair containing diphthongal words with contrasting visible speech movements.	To lead the student to make his own deductions regarding the visible aspects of the diphthongs and indirectly of other vowels.

Film Number	Phonetic Content	Script Content	Objectives
VII (Female Speaker)	Homophonous words (words having identical visible speech aspects).	Series of two or more unrelated sentences, each containing words differing in sound and spelling but having identical visible characteristics.	To achieve visual alertness in detecting, discriminating, and memorizing the visibly identical phenomena which make one word look like another.
VIII (Female Speaker)	Group I of the post-dental sibilant consonants: [s] as in "seal" [z] as in "zeal"	Unrelated sentences in which these consonants occur frequently.	To familiarize the student with the varying visible speech characteristics of [s] and [z], when preceded or followed by vowels of widely different appearance.
IX (Female Speaker)	The lingua-dental consonants: [θ] as in "thin" [ð] as in "then" contrasted with [m], [ʍ], [f] and [v],	Series of three unrelated sentences are spoken. In each group one sentence contains a predominance of [θ] and [ð], another of [ʍ] and [w] and a third of [f] and [v].	To develop sharpness of discrimination by requiring the student to analyze, contrast, and differentiate visible speech clues as they actually occur in speech.
X (Male Speaker)	Review of phonetic elements developed in Films I to IX.	Isolated unrelated sentences in each of which occur frequently one or more of the following consonants: [ʍ], [w], [p], [b], [m], [f], [v], [θ], [ð].	To exercise visual memory by recall of the visible clues observed in previous assignments and to recognize them in new words and changed sentence structure. This film may be used as a visual hearing test.
XI (Female Speaker)	Group II of post-dental fricatives: [ʃ] as in "sheep" [tʃ] as in "cheap" [dʒ] as in "jeep"	Unrelated sentences in each of which occur frequently [ʃ], [tʃ], or [dʒ].	To analyze the visible aspects of these consonants and to observe their somewhat varying appearance as influenced by preceding and succeeding vowels.

Film Number	*Phonetic Content*	*Script Content*	*Objectives*
XII (Female Speaker)	Homophonous sentences.	Groups of two or more sentences nearly alike in appearance.	To develop skill in differentiating through context between similar sets of visual clues.
XIII (Female Speaker)	The lateral post-dental continuant: [l] as in *"love"*	Five sentences and four poems in which this consonant occurs frequently in initial, medial, and final positions.	To provide practice in following varying visible rhythmic speech patterns. The longer units of sustained thought in poetry assist in developing the ability to synthesize.
XIV (Male Speaker)	The post-dental stop plosive consonants: [t] as in *"tear"* [d] as in *"dear"* and the post-dental nasal continuant, [n] as in *"near"*	Unrelated sentences in each of which one of these consonants occurs frequently.	To observe and analyze these somewhat visibly obscure consonants as their appearance is affected by preceding and succeeding vowels and consonants.
XV (Female Speaker)	Phrasing, intonation, and stress.	Four short stories.	To increase the power to synthesize through: 1. Prolonged attention span. 2. Retention of visible clues. 3. Thought interpretation from facial expression.
XVI (Female Speaker)	The post-dental fricative continuant consonant: [r] as in *"run"*	Unrelated sentences in which the consonant [r] occurs repeatedly in initial, medial, and final positions.	To study the visible characteristic changes this consonant undergoes under the influence of preceding and succeeding vowels and consonants.
XVII (Female Speaker)	The post-dental fricative consonants combination [r] blends: [pr] as in *"pride"* [br] as in *"bride"* [kr] as in *"cried"* etc.	Unrelated sentences, each containing several of the various [r] combinations.	To study the visible changes affecting this consonant when preceded by other consonants

Film Number	Phonetic Content	Script Content	Objectives
XVIII (Female Speaker)	All forms of the consonant [r].	Nine poems in which this consonant occurs in various forms.	To develop the ability to synthesize through the rhythmic context of poetry.
XIX (Female Speaker)	The post-dental fricative consonants [ʒ] and [ʃ] as in "azure" and in various word endings: tion, sien, teous, tious, tient, tience, etc.	Numbered sentences featuring the consonants [ʒ] and [ʃ] and these various word endings. Each sentence discusses some aspect of the nursing profession.	To develop a larger visual vocabulary and a longer visual memory span through recognition of visible clues in longer thought units.
XX (Male Speaker)	Review of all phonetic principles presented in Films I to XIX.	Unrelated sentences of greater length and difficulty than those in Film X.	Same as for Film X. This film may be used as a visual hearing test.
XXI (Female Speaker)	Three palatal consonants: [k] as in "*k*illed" [g] as in "*g*uild" [ŋ] as in "ki*ng*"	Unrelated sentences in which three consonants occur frequently in initial, medial, and final positions.	To teach alert perception of these visibly obscure sounds when occurring in conjunction with various preceding and succeeding vowels and consonants.
XXII (Female Speaker)	The post-dental lateral continuant in combination: [dl] as in "can*dle*"	Fifteen quotations from various sources in which the words "candle" and "candle-light" occur frequently.	To enrich the observer's cultural background by acquainting him with a form of literary expression differing from his own daily conversational pattern.
XXIII (Female Speaker)	Sibilant consonant combinations: [st] as in "*st*ate" [sk] as in "*sk*ate"	Connected thought in topic form. The speaker talks about Florida.	1. To increase the visual memory span. 2. To increase the retention of visual memory images. 3. To enlarge the visual vocabulary.

Film Number	*Phonetic Content*	*Script Content*	*Objectives*
XXIV (Female Speaker)	The phonetic problem of visual recognition of proper names.	Each unrelated sentence describes a geographical place.	To provide practice in the visual perception of terms which the majority of acoustically handicapped persons finds difficult.
XXV (Male Speaker)	Review of the bilabials [p], [b], and [m], bi-labial combinations: [pr] as in "*pr*ay" [pl] as in "*pl*ay" [br] as in "*br*ew" [bl] as in "*bl*ew"	Paragraphs discussing wild game. Photographs serve as visual aids.	To provide interesting educational descriptions that aid in the acquisition of a varied visual vocabulary.
XXVI (Female Speaker)	Labio-dental combinations: [fl] as in "*fl*ee" [fr] as in "*fr*ee"	The speaker talks about Arizona.	Same as the objectives in Film XXV.
XXVII (Female Speaker)	The rhythm of song.	Songs of various rhythms and tempos sung by a trained voice.	To relate the previously learned patterns of speech to the tempo of singing.
XXVIII (Male Speaker)	The palatals [k], [g], and [ŋ] reviewed and various combinations featured. [kl] as in "en*cl*osed" [kr] as in "*cr*eated" [gr] as in "Con*gr*ess" [gl] as in "En*gl*and"	The speaker talks about the Library of Congress.	Same as the objectives in Film XXV.
XXIX (Female Speaker)	The glottal fricative consonant: [h] as in "*h*ome"	The speaker talks about Ohio.	To present for visual analysis the consonant [h] followed by different vowels.
XXX (Male Speaker)	Review of all phonetic principles presented in Films I to XXIX.	Longer and more difficult sentences than those in review Films X and XX.	To give the student some indication of his progress in visual speech comprehension. This film may be used as a test.

The films may be purchased from the Department of Photography, Brown Hall, Ohio State University, Columbus 10, Ohio, or rented for a short period from the Department of Speech, Derby Hall, Ohio State University, Columbus 10, Ohio.

APPENDIX C

PRACTICE ACTIVITIES

THE FOLLOWING TEN ACTIVITIES ARE SUGGESTIVE OF THE TYPE THAT MIGHT BE incorporated into lipreading lesson plans. These activities have been successfully employed in lipreading lessons for adults and children. The creative therapist should encounter little difficulty in formulating additional activities.

FOR ADULTS

Materials	*Procedures*
1. Pictures of six scenic areas of the U.S.A.	Place pictures on the wall. Present a short description of each picture. Have case select the picture that has been described.
2. Article from newspaper.	Write key words on the blackboard. Read the article. Ask questions to determine whether case understood what was read.
3. Twenty cards (5″ x 8″) with a word printed on each card.	Therapist tapes the cards in two rows of ten each to the mirror. The rows are two feet apart. Case sits on a chair between the rows facing the mirror. Therapist stands behind case and says sentences in which one of the words is employed. Case points to the word used.
4. Pictures such as found on *Saturday Evening Post* covers.	Pictures are shown to the case for a short period of time and then removed. The therapist questions the case as to the details of the picture.
5. Pictures showing sports, as golf, tennis, swimming, baseball, basketball, football, and so forth.	Therapist says a sentence such as, "He hit a home run." Case identifies the sport.

Materials	*Procedures*
1. Pictures that illustrate nursery rhymes.	Start a rhyme and then stop and see if child can pick up where therapist left off.
2. Pictures of animate and inanimate objects.	Therapist shows one picture at a time to the case and asks questions about the picture that can be answered with a number. For example, "How many wheels are on the car?"—"How many eyes does the horse have?"—and so forth.
3. A tour around the school.	When case and therapist return to the room the therapist asks the child questions such as, "Where did we see the water fountain?"—and so forth.
4. Pictures of objects (house, church, grocery store, service station, bakery, post office, bank, and so on).	Therapist pretends to be a visitor and case is the guide. The therapist requests to be taken to many places about the town. Case shows him where these places are located.
5. Toy store.	Therapist is customer and case is clerk. Therapist requests items and case takes them from shelf.

INDEX

A

Adult assignments:
  communication environments, 119
  communication patterns, 119
  directed reading, 122
  examples, 120-122
  home television, 120
  self attitudes, 119
  situational practice, 122
  three areas, 118-119
Advice to parents:
  basic information, 124-125
  behavior dynamics, 125
  child's hearing aid, 125-126
  distinction between "deaf" and "hard of hearing," 125
  materials, 125, 126
Allport, F. H., 3
American Annals of the Deaf, 13, 15
American Hearing Society, 122, 128
American Instructors of the Deaf, 15
American Society for the Hard of Hearing, 89
American Speech and Hearing Association, 128-129

Amman, J. C., 11
Analytic approach:
  Bruhn method, 85
  diagram, 2
Aristotle, 10
Armstrong, M. B., 72
Association, defined, 4
Attention span, through use of visual aids, 51
Auditory tolerance, development, 72
Auditory training:
  equipment reference levels, 73
  goals, 78
  mirror amplification, 77
  use of filters, 77
Aural rehabilitation:
  examples, 79-81
  vital factors, 71
Ausherman, M., 32

B

Baker, H., 11, 12
Bangs, Tina E., 72
Barnette, G. C., 54

Bartlett, Ruth, 51
Bell, A. G., 11, 14
Bell, Mrs. A. G., 15, 16
Bell, Melville, 14, 15
Black, J. W., 32, 56, 74
Blakeley, Robert W., 43
Bonaparte, Napoleon, 15
Bonet, J. P., 10
Braidwood, John, 13
Braidwood, T., 13
Brannon, Jr., John B., 47
Braukmann, K., 17, 88, 96
Browd, Victor L., 73
Bruhn, Martha, 16, 17, 51, 85, 95
Bulwer, J., 10
Bunger, A., 17, 84, 88, 96
Byers, V. W., 48

C

Canfield, Norton, 122, 128
Cardan, J., 10
Carter, Jr., C. W., 32
Case-Ruch Test of Spatial Relations, 41,
    48, 55
Cavender, Betty J., 38
Children's assignments:
    examples, 123-124
    goals, 122
    role of parents, 122-123
Clarke, John, 14
Clarke School for the Deaf, 14, 24
Clerc, Laurent, 14
Clinician, suggested meaning, 8
Closed circuit television (*see also* Tele-
    vision):
    cost of equipment, 138
    description of program, 134, 138
    equipment, 138
    use in lipreading, 136
Closure:
    defined, 55
    practice, 55
Cobbs, Virginia, 13
Combined practice:
    phonetic approach, 76
    story retention, 76
    suggested approach, 75-76
Commercial television (*see also* Tele-
    vision):
    advantages, 136

Commercial television (*cont.*)
    description of possible program, 137
    problems, 137
Conklin, E. S., 22, 23
Council for Exceptional Children, 129
Crawley, Edward F., 131
Curry, E. T., 72
Cypresasen, Lucile, 131

D

Dale, E., 32
Dalgarno, G., 11
Davidson, J.L., 38, 40, 41, 42
Davis, H., 122, 128
Day, H. E., 23
Deland, F., 9, 14
Delayed auditory feedback:
    description, 49
    effect upon lipreading, 44-45
de l'Epee, C. M., 12
Deshon Book, The, 102
Dewey, G., 32
DiCarlo, Louis M., 27, 78
Dreher, J. J., 74

E

Efron, David, 57
Egan, James P., 74
Equipment, for combined training, 72
Exercises, for combined training, 73
Eye training, suggestions by Nitchie, 50, 51

F

Fabregas, M. B., 89
Faircloth, M., 104
Fay, E. H., 10

Feilbach, R. V., 91, 104
Figure-ground recognition, training, 52
Films (*see* Mason, Morkovin, Moser, State University of Iowa Department of Otolaryngology)
Fisher, M., 104
Fossum, E. C., 32
Fragmentary sentences, 49
Fraprie, F. R., 32
French, N. R., 32
Fusfeld, I. S., 23

G

Galambos, R., 6
Gallaudet, Thomas, 13
Gardner, H. J., 28
Gault, Robert, 42
Glorig, Aram, 51
Goetzinger, C. R., 44
Graded materials (*see* Kinzie)
Green, C., 13
Green, F., 13
Guilford-Zimmerman Temperament Survey, 40

H

Hanfmann and Kasanin Test, 41, 49
Hartford, Connecticut, 14
Hearing aid:
  child's hearing aid, 125-126
  use in combined practice, 77
Heider, F. K., 23, 38
Heider, G. M., 23, 38
Heinicke, S., 12
Hempen, C., 134
Historical aspects of lipreading:
  early development in America:
    American Annals of the Deaf, 13, 15
    American Instructors of the Deaf, 15
    Bell, M., 14, 15
    Braidwood, J., 13
    Clarke, J., 14
    Clarke School for the Deaf, 14, 24
    Clerc, Laurent, 14

Historical aspects of lipreading (*cont.*)
  early development in America (*cont.*)
    Cobbs, Virginia, 13
    Deland, F., 9, 14
    Gallaudet, T., 13
    Hartford, Connecticut, 14
    Luzerne, R., 13
    Mann, H., 14
    Northampton, Massachusetts, 14
    Peet, H. P., 13
    Timberlake, J. B., 12
    Turner, W. W., 14
    Volta Review, 15
    Warren, L., 15
  early development in Europe:
    Aristotle, 10
    Bonet, J. P., 10
    Bulwer, J., 10
    Cardan, J., 10
    Dalgarno, G., 11
    Lucretius, 10
    Ponce de Leon, P., 10
  more recent development in America:
    Bell, Mrs. A. G., 15, 16
    Brauckmann, K., 17, 88
    Bruhn, M., 16, 17, 85
    Kinzie, C. E., 16
    Kinzie, R., 16
    Mason, M. K., 18, 24, 31
    Moore, L., 18
    Morkovin, B. V., 18, 26
    New York League for the Hard of Hearing, 16
    Nitchie, E. B., 15, 16, 22, 23
    Nitchie, Mrs. E. B., 17
    Reighard, J., 17
    Whittaker, B., 17
  more recent development in Europe:
    Amman, J. C., 11
    Baker, H., 11, 12
    Bell, A. G., 11, 14
    Braidwood, T., 13
    de l'Epee, C. M., 12
    Green, C., 13
    Green, F., 13
    Heinicke, S., 12
    Periere, J. R., 12
    Sicard, Abbe, 12
  present status:
    effects of World War II, 19
    in the U.S.A., 19
    Veterans Administration program, 19
Home assignments:
  attitudinal, 118
  disadvantages, 118
  when suggested, 117
Hoverstein, G., 128

Hudgins, C. V., 71
Hutton, Charles, 72

I

Instructor:
    characteristics for television, 139
    considerations in presentation, 8
    requirements, 7
    training, 8
Iowa, State University of, Department of
    Otolaryngology, 28

J

Jena, Germany, 17
Jena method, (*see* Brauckmann)
John Tracy Clinic, 28, 37, 43
Johnson, Elizabeth H., 71
Johnson, Wendell, *quoted,* 6

K

Kaho, Elizabeth E., 132
Katja, R., 27
Keaster, J., 128
Kees, W., 57
Kelly, J. C., 27, 73
Kinzie, Cora E., 16, 93, 96
Kinzie method (*see* Kinzie)
Kinzie, Rose, 16, 93, 96
Kitson, H. D., 22, 37, 41
Knower-Dusenbury Test, 39, 40, 49
Knower Speech Attitude Scale, 39, 49
Kodman, Jr., Frank, 47
Koenig, Jr., W., 32

L

Larr, Alfred L., 134
Larsen Consonant Discrimination Test, 74
Larsen, Laila, 74
Leavis, M. H., 90
Lehman, A., 88
Lesson planning:
    discussion of cases, 107-116
    suggestions for, 116
    underlying rationale, 106, 107
Level of aspiration, 40
Lieberman, L., 48
Lip movements:
    photographs, 59-67
    use of photographs, 57
Lipreader, requirements, 7
Lipreading:
    definition, 2
    end goal, 2
    form of perceptual behavior, 3
    form of learned behavior, 3
    in information theory terminology, 56
    learning strange vocabulary, 4
    philosophy, 8
    problems, 50
    three factors for success, 50
Lipreading ability:
    and ability to interpret incomplete pat-
        terns of speech, 43
    and behavioral patterns, 39, 40
    and difficulty of stimulus, 44-47
    and intelligence, 37, 38
    and listening ability, 43
    and reading ability, 42
    and related factors, 37
    and speaker, 47-48
    and tactual stimulation, 42
    and viewing distance, 44
    and visual-motor coordination, 41
    and visual skills, 40-42
Lipreading training:
    goals, 7, 8
    use of cartoons, 57
    use of magazine covers, 56, 57
    use of slides and filmstrips, 57
Listening:
    described, 6
    factors related to, 6
    neurophysiological aspects, 6
    tests, 83
Lorge, I., 32
Lowell, Edgar L., 28, 43
Lucretius, 10
Luzerne, Rae, 13

M

McBride, Jack, 131
Macnutt, E., 91
Mann, Horace, 14
Mason, Marie K., 5, 18, 24, 31, 47, 101, 141, 147
Mason films, use in training, 68, 69 (*see also* Appendix B)
Materials:
  consonants, 74
  monosyllabic words, 74
  polysyllabic words, 74
  recorded, 82
  requirements, 7
Meaning, development, 2
Methods and materials:
  for adults:
    Brauckmann, K., 96
    Bruhn, M., 95
    Bunger, A., 96
    Deshon Book, The, 102
    Faircloth, M., 104
    Feilbach, R. V., 104
    Fisher, M., 104
    Kinzie, Cora, 96
    Kinzie, Rose, 96
    Mason films, 68, 69 (*see also* Appendix B)
    Mason, M. K., 101
    Montague, H., 102
    Morgenstern, L. I., 100, 101
    Morkovin, B. V., 102
    Moore, L., 102
    Nitchie, E. B., 93
    Ordman, K. A., 103
    Ralli, M. P., 103
    Synthetic approach, 94
    Whittaker, B., 96
  for children:
    Brauckmann, K., 88
    Bruhn, M., 85
    Fabregas, M. B., 89
    Feilbach, R. V., 91
    Kinzie, C., 86
    Kinzie, R., 86
    Leavis, M. H., 90
    Lehman, A., 88
    Macnutt, E., 91
    Mason multiple choice tests (*see* Appendix A)
    Morkovin films, 91, 92
    movement words, 87
    New aids and materials, 89

Methods and materials (*cont.*)
  for children (*cont.*)
    Samuelson, E. E., 88, 89
    Scally, M. A., 88
    Stowell, A., 88
    syllable drill, 85
    Whildin, O. A., 88
    Whitehurst, M. W., 92
    W.P.A. project, 89
    Yenrick, D. E., 90, 91
Miller, J., 44
Minski, L., 29
Mirror practice, 94, 118
Montague, Harriet, 9, 102
Moore, Lucelia, 18, 91, 102, 131
Moore, W. E., 56
Morgenstern, L. I., 100, 101
Morkovin, B. V., 18, 26, 91, 92, 102
Morkovin films, use in training, 68, 69
Morris, Dorothy M., 44-45
Moser, H. M., 29, 31, 74
Motion pictures:
  Mason films, 68, 69 (*see also* Appendix B)
  Morkovin films, 68, 69
  use in training, 69
Movement words, 87
Mueller-Walle, H. J., 16
Mulligan, Marigene, 43
Myklebust, H. R., 128

N

Neely, Keith K., 46
New Aids and Materials for Teaching Lip-reading, 89
New York League for the Hard of Hearing, 16
Nichols, R. G., 5-6
Nitchie, E. B., 15, 16, 22, 23, 50, 93
Nitchie, Mrs. E. B., 17
Northampton, Massachusetts, 14
Numbers, Mary E., 71

O

Ohio State University:
  psychological examination, 38
  test of lipreading, 28

O'Neill, John J., 28, 31, 38, 39, 40, 41, 42, 45, 47, 132
Ordman, Kathryn, 103, 133
Orthotelephonic:
    materials, 73
    in auditory training, 73
Osgood, C. E., *quoted*, 2
Oyer, H. J., 21, 28, 31, 74

P

Parental conferences:
    examples, 126
    home assignments, 128
    purposes, 126
    reading assignments, 128
Pauls, M. D., 25, 47
Peet, H. P., 13
Perceptual field, 52
Periere, J. R., 12
Peripheral field, 52
Philadelphia, Pennsylvania, 17
Pilot television program, 139
Pintner, R., 23, 38
Pollack, I., 45
Ponce de Leon, Pedro, 10
Porter, J., 125
Practice activities:
    adults, 154
    children, 155
Preparatory set, 4
Pre-structuring, 5
Primary Mental Abilities Test, 40

Q

Quick, Marian, 71

R

Ralli, Mary P., 103, 133
Raven's Progressive Matrices, 55

Reams, Mary H., 46
Reighard, J., 17
Reinforcement, 5
Renshaw, S., 54
Reid, Gladys, 26, 38
Research, possible areas:
    effects of environment, 44
    personality factors, 40-41
    stimulus materials, 47
    visual, 42
    visual skills, 40
Ronnei, Eleanor C., 125
Rotter Incomplete Sentence Test, 39, 40
Rotter Level of Aspiration Test, 40, 49
Rousey, C. L., 44
Ruesch, Jurgen, 57

S

Samuelson, E. E., 88, 89
Scally, M. A., 88
Scrambled words, practice, 55
Shapley, James L., 72
Sicard, Abbe, 12
Simmons, Audrey A., 38, 41, 42, 43, 49
Speech reading, defined, 47
Speech thinking, defined, 39
Speech-to-noise ratio, in combined practice, 75
Stephens, M. C., 22
Stevens, L. A., 5-6
Stimulus materials, manner of presentation, 8
Stobschinski, Robert, 39
Stone, Louis, 48
Stowell, A., 88
Suci, G. J., *quoted*, 2
Sumby, W. H., 45
Syllable drill, 85
Synthetic ability, 52
Synthetic approach, *diagram*, 2
    Nitchie method, 94

T

Taaffe, Gordon, 45
Tachistoscope:
    description, 53
    use in training, 51, 53, 54

Tachistoscopic recognition, 37, 41
Tannenbaum, P. H., *quoted*, 2
Teaching of lipreading, three areas of consideration, 7
Television:
    closed circuit, 134, 136, 138
    commercial, 136, 137
    instruction, 69, 130
    programs, 131, 132, 133, 134, 135, 136, 139
Tests of combined practice, 71, 72
Tests of lipreading:
    factors to consider in the construction of:
        conditions, 33
        format, 31
        item selection, 32
        population to be tested, 30, 31
        scoring the test, 33
        speakers, 31
    purpose of, 20, 21
    review of:
        Cavender, B. J., 27
        Conklin, E. S., 22, 23
        Day, H. E., 23
        Fusfeld, I. S., 23
        Heider, F. K., 23
        Heider, G. M., 23
        Kelly, J. C., 27
        Kitson, M. D., 22
        Lowell, E., 28
        Mason, M. K., 24
        Minski, L., 29
        Ohio State Test, 28
        Pintner, R., 23
        Reid, G., 26
        Stephens, M. C., 22
        Wright, J. D., 23
    Tests of lipreading ability:
        effects upon research, 36
        face to face test, 38
        filmed tests, 38, 42, 43, 45, 46
Thorndike, E. L., 32
Timberlake, Josephine B., 12
Turner, W. W., 14

V

Variables, in experimental study of lipreading, 35
Veterans Administration program, 19

Visibility:
    consonants, 45, 46
    vowels, 45
    words, 45, 47
Visual awareness, teaching of, 51
Visual concentration:
    method of improving, 57
    use of skits or charades, 57, 68
Visual form training, purposes, 56
Visual hearing:
    defined, 5, 47
    films (*see* Appendix B)
    tests for children (*see* Appendix A)
Visual listening, definition, 5, 6
Visual memory span, definition, 49
Visual perception, practice, 52
Visual skill, areas to be explored, 52
Visual thought comprehension, 2
Visual training, carry-over, 68
Voelker, C. H., 28, 29, 32
Volta Bureau, 9, 15, 128
Volta Prize, 15
Volta Review, 15

W

Walker, Crayton, 74
Warren, Lillie, 15
Wechsler-Bellevue test, 38, 41
Wedenburg, E., 77
Whildin, C. A., 88
Whitehurst, M. W., 92
Whittaker, B., 17, 96
Wong, Wilson, 45
Woodward, Mary F., 46
Wooley, Florence T. W., 51
W.P.A. project in lipreading, 89
Word guessing:
    description, 56
    in lipreading training, 56
Worthington, A. M., 40
Wright, J. D., 23

Y

Yenrick, D. E., 90, 91

DATE DUE